MURDER & MAYHEM
IN CHICAGO'S
DOWNTOWN

MURDER & MAYHEM IN CHICAGO'S DOWNTOWN

TROY TAYLOR

Charleston · London

THE
History
PRESS

Published by The History Press
Charleston, SC 29403
www.historypress.net

Copyright © 2009 by Troy Taylor
All rights reserved

First published 2009

Manufactured in the United States

ISBN 978.1.59629.694.7

Library of Congress Cataloging-in-Publication Data

Taylor, Troy.
Murder and mayhem in Chicago's downtown / Troy Taylor.
p. cm.
Includes bibliographical references.
ISBN 978-1-59629-694-7
1. Murder--Illinois--Chicago--History--Anecdotes. 2. Crime--Illinois--Chicago-
-History--Anecdotes. 3. Criminals--Illinois--Chicago--Biography--Anecdotes.
4. Chicago (Ill.)--History--Anecdotes. 5. Chicago (Ill.)--Biography--Anecdotes. 6.
Chicago (Ill.)--Social conditions--Anecdotes. I. Title.
HV6534.C4T38 2009
364.152'3092277311--dc22
2009037770

CONTENTS

Acknowledgements

I would like to thank the many writers and chroniclers of crime in the Windy City, especially Herbert Asbury, Jay Robert Nash and Richard Lindberg, and the kind keepers of libraries, history rooms and archives who always went out of their way to help. Thanks also to Jonathan Simcosky at The History Press and my wife, Haven, for putting up with a lot of strange interests and for her patience during numerous side trips to crime scenes and murder sites.

INTRODUCTION

There are many who believe that a dark pall hangs over the downtown area of Chicago. This part of the city has long been a place of horror, crime, tragedy and death, dating back to the earliest days of the Fort Dearborn Massacre and continuing with the Great Chicago Fire in 1871. Unfortunately, those horrific events were not the only times that Chicago was marked by disaster. Over the decades, the city has seen more than its share.

Fires have taken many lives in Chicago and left a vivid mark on the city. While the Great Chicago Fire was the most famous blaze in the city's history, it was certainly not the only time that the city was scorched with flames. Numerous other infernos have singed the face of Chicago over the decades, but perhaps the most tragic occurred downtown in 1903, when hundreds were killed during the Iroquois Theatre disaster. This remains one of the most devastating theatre fires in American history, and the deaths that occurred there could be directly traced back to political graft, greed and criminal negligence.

The Iroquois Theatre, the newest and most beautiful showplace in Chicago in 1903, was believed to be "absolutely fireproof," according to newspaper reports. The *Chicago Tribune* called it a "virtual temple of beauty," but just five weeks after it opened, it became a blazing deathtrap.

Downtown Chicago at Dearborn and
Randolph Streets in 1909. *Courtesy of the*
Chicago Daily News.

The Iroquois Theatre on the fateful morning of December 30, 1903.

The new theatre was much acclaimed, even before it was unveiled to the public. It was patterned after the Opéra Comique in Paris and was located downtown on the north side of Randolph Street, between State and Dearborn Streets. The interior of the four-story building was magnificent, with stained glass and polished wood throughout. The lobby had an ornate sixty-foot ceiling and featured white marble walls fitted with large mirrors that were framed in gold leaf and stone. Two grand staircases led away from either side of the lobby to the balcony areas. Outside, the building's façade resembled a Greek temple, with a towering stone archway supported by massive columns.

Thanks to the dozens of fires that had occurred over the years in theatres, architect Benjamin H. Marshall wanted to assure the public that the Iroquois was safe. He studied a number of fires that had occurred in the past and made every effort to make sure that no tragedy would occur in the new theatre. The Iroquois had twenty-five exits that, it was claimed, could empty the building in less than five minutes. The stage had also been fitted with an asbestos curtain that could be quickly lowered to protect the audience.

While all of this was impressive, it was not enough to battle the real problems that existed in the Iroquois. Seats in the theatre were wooden, with cushions stuffed with hemp, and much of the precautionary fire equipment that was to have been installed never actually made it into the building. The theatre had no fire alarms, and in a rush to open on time, other safety factors had been forgotten or simply ignored.

The horrific fire occurred on the bitterly cold afternoon of December 30, 1903. A holiday crowd had packed into the theatre on that Wednesday afternoon to see a matinée performance of the hit vaudeville comedy *Mr. Bluebeard*. Officially, the Iroquois seated 1,602 people, with approximately 700 in the expensive "parquet" (the seats down in front that overlooked the orchestra pit), more than 400 in the first balcony and probably just under 500 in the steep upper balcony. There were four lower boxes, each seating six people, and two upper boxes designed to hold four people each, but the owners had managed to crowd eight chairs into those boxes.

Added to those who had purchased tickets to the show in advance were the usual late arrivals. Some came to buy tickets for available standing room; others had guest passes from connections they had with the management, contractors, actors and theatre employees. Others had been given tickets by city inspectors who had done favors for the owners of the theatre. Estimates vary, but because the managers wanted to make up for earlier, smaller shows, there may have been considerably more than 200 standees that afternoon. By curtain time, an estimated 1,840 people, most of them women and children, were packed into the house. This was far beyond capacity. The overflow had people filling the seats and standing four deep in the aisles. Another crowd filled the backstage area with 400 actors, dancers and stagehands.

As the show was about to begin, actor and star of the show Eddie Foy was delighted at the size of the crowd. "That Wednesday afternoon, the house was packed and many were standing," he later said. "I was struck by the fact that I had never seen so many women and children. Even the gallery was full." What Foy did not see beyond the bright stage lights was that the Iroquois auditorium was not merely full, but also dangerously overcrowded. One usher would later claim that there were at least five hundred people standing in the auditorium.

Anticipation mounted as the lights dimmed for the show's first act. In accordance with the owner's standard operating procedures, most of the doors leading from the balcony and gallery had been locked by the ushers to keep out gate crashers and prevent those sitting or standing in the upper tiers from sneaking down in the darkness to the more expensive seats. This was done regardless of the fact that it was obvious that there were no empty seats anywhere.

The audience was thrilled with the show's first act. During intermission, those in the expensive sections and boxes retired to the smoking room or went to freshen up, relax on the plush couches and mingle on the promenade. Those in the balcony and gallery, behind the locked and bolted gates, flowed through the upper promenade and used the restrooms.

By 3:20 p.m., the second act of *Mr. Bluebeard* was well underway. During one of the early scenes, possibly while Foy was riding a baby elephant, Nellie Reed of the aerial ballet was hooked to a thin trolley wire that sent her high above the audience during a musical number. The sequence was made spectacular through the use of hundreds of colored lights. Some of the bulbs were concealed inside two narrow concave metal reflectors located on each side of the stage. Called front lighting, each reflector was mounted on vertical hinges and, when not needed, was supposed to be pivoted by stagehands

Eddie Foy, a popular stage actor and the star of *Mr. Bluebeard* at the Iroquois Theatre.

so that it disappeared into a niche in the wall. The lights were not needed for the number that was about to start, but for some reason a member of the stage crew had not retracted the right stage reflector. It was left slightly extended, and one edge of it was in the path of the curtains. In the usual business of moving scenery, adjusting lights, moving backdrops and the hundreds of other things that needed to be done, no one noticed the error.

In the scene that followed, all of the houselights were extinguished, bathing the stage in a soft blue glow from one of the backstage carbon arc lamps, a powerful spotlight that was created by an electric current arcing between two carbon rods. The spotlight was positioned on a narrow metal bridge that was about fifteen feet above the stage and within a foot or so of the theatre's drop curtains and the fixed curtain that prevented the audience from seeing into the wings. The spotlight was a bulky piece of machinery, with a large metal hood and reflector, and could generate temperatures as high as four thousand degrees Fahrenheit.

As the action continued on the stage, bringing beautiful chorus girls and young men in uniform into the softly lit gardens, the carbon arc lamp suddenly began to sputter and spark. A cracking sound was heard, and then a few inches of orange flame appeared and began to spread out, dancing along the edge of the fixed curtain. On the stage below, the cast went into an up-tempo song as stagehands tried to slap at the small flame with their bare hands. Within seconds, the tiny blaze had grown, consuming the material above their heads and beyond their reach. It was soon spreading into the heavier curtains, and they shouted to a man on a catwalk above to try and put out the fire. He also began slapping at the fire with his hands.

The audience was engrossed in the romantic musical number onstage as on either side of the garden set, stagehands, grips and those on the catwalks frantically tried to get to the fire and put it out. But the flames had grown larger and were out of reach. Black smoke was starting to rise.

William Sallers, the house fireman, was on his usual rounds to make sure that no one was smoking, and as he made his way up the stairs from the dressing rooms in the basement, he spotted the flames. He immediately grabbed some tubes of Kilfyre (a powdery flame retardant), ran up the vertical stairs of the light bridge and began frantically tossing powder onto the growing fire. The platform was only eighteen inches wide, so he had to hold on to a metal rail with one hand as he threw the powder with the other. But it was too late. The flames had spread to the point that the small amount of powder was almost comically ineffectual.

At first, the actors onstage had no idea what was happening, but after a few sparks began to rain down on them, they knew something was seriously wrong. They continued to sing and dance, waiting for something to happen. Later, some of the actors recalled hearing shouts and bells that signaled for the curtain to come down, but they were muffled by the music.

In the orchestra pit, the musicians spotted the fire and an order was given for them to play as fast as they could. The tempo picked up but soon faltered as more of the musicians spotted the flames and became rattled. Several of them calmly put down their instruments and exited through the orchestra pit door beneath the stage.

Depending on where they were sitting or standing, some members of the audience saw the fire as they followed the gaze of the actors, who were now looking up. At first, many of them were merely puzzled, but others became alarmed. Most of the children in the front main floor rows remained in their seats, believing that the glow that was spreading across the upper reaches of the theatre was another of the show's magical effects.

Those in the upper gallery who saw the eerie flickering of flames had no idea at first what was happening, until bits of burning fabric began falling down around members of the cast, who were still trying to go on with their number. It was becoming obvious that some of them had fallen out of step with the music, and others seemed to have lost their voices. Most were terribly frightened, but survivors of the fire later claimed that seeing those girls remaining there, still dancing in an effort to quiet the audience, was one of the bravest acts they had ever witnessed.

Backstage, things became more frightening and chaotic. The stage manager, William Carelton, could not be found (he had gone to the hardware store), and one of the stagehands, Joe Dougherty, was trying to handle the curtains from near the switchboard. Dougherty was filling in for the regular curtain man, who was in the hospital, and could not remember which drop should be lowered. The asbestos curtain ran on an endless loop of wire-enforced rope, but he was not sure which rope controlled the curtain.

High above him, Charles Sweeney, who had been assigned to the first fly gallery, seized a canvas tarpaulin and, with some of the other men, was slapping at the flames. The fire was out of their reach, however, and it continued to spread. Sweeney dashed down six flights of stairs to a room filled with chorus girls and led them down to a small stage exit. In the rush to escape, most of the girls dropped everything and left the building wearing only flimsy costumes or tights. Other men raced downstairs to rescue girls who were in the dressing rooms under the stage.

High up in the theatre's gridiron, the Grigolatis, a group of sixteen young German aerialists (twelve women and four men), had a horrifying view of the scene. Clouds of thick, black smoke were rising toward them, and blazing pieces of canvas the size of bedsheets were falling down on the stage and the footlights. William Sallers, still above the stage, knew that the theatre was doomed.

The Grigolatis had only seconds to act. One of them, Floraline, who was perched some distance away from the others, was suddenly engulfed in flames from a burning piece of scenery. Before the others could reach her, she panicked, lost her grip on the trapeze and plunged to the stage, sixty feet below. By the time her companions were able to unhook themselves from their harnesses and scramble down some metal scaffolding to the stage, Floraline had vanished. They could only hope that she had been carried to safety.

In all of the confusion, no one remembered aerialist Nellie Reed, who was still attached to her wire.

In one of the dressing rooms, five young female dancers were sitting and talking when they heard the cries of "fire!" In the rush to get out, one of them, Violet Sidney, twisted her ankle and fell. The other girls ran, but Lola Quinlan stopped to help Violet. She managed to drag Violet down five flights of stairs and across the back of the burning stage to safety. Lola was badly burned in the process, but she refused to leave her friend behind.

Voices screamed for the asbestos curtain to come down, but nothing happened. Joe Dougherty and others were still confused about which curtains should be lowered, and more time was lost. A stagehand who had been ordered to sound the fire alarm found that no alarm box had ever been installed. He burst out of the theatre and ran as fast as he could through the streets to notify Engine Company 13 of the blaze.

Inside his dressing room, Eddie Foy, in tights, misshapen shoes, a short smock and a red pigtailed wig, was preparing for his novelty act as the Old Woman Who Lived in a Shoe. Foy heard the commotion outside and rushed out onto the stage to see what was going on. As soon as he opened the door, he knew that something was deadly wrong. He immediately searched for his young son, who had accompanied him to the theatre that day, and quickly found him in the darkness. As he stumbled with the boy in his arms, he heard terrified voices raising a cry of "fire!" At that moment, the nearly two thousand people packed into the "absolutely fireproof" Iroquois Theatre began to panic.

Some of the audience had risen to their feet; others were running and climbing over the seats to get to the back of the house and to the side exits. Many of the standees were blocking the aisles and, since the new theatre was unfamiliar to them, were unsure about which way to turn. The initial runners soon turned into a mob that was trying to get out the same way it had come in. Their screams and cries were muffled by the music and by the cast members who were still singing as the burning scenery fell around them. Terrified families were quickly torn apart.

Eddie Foy grabbed his son and rushed to the stage exit, but he felt compelled to go back inside. He pressed the boy into the arms of a fleeing stagehand and went back to try and help calm down the audience and finally bring the curtain down. By the time he arrived, the cast had abandoned the stage, and he stood there alone, the blazing backdrop behind him and burning bits of scenery raining down around him. Smoke billowed as he stepped to the edge of the footlights, still partially clothed in his ridiculous costume. He urged everyone who could hear him to remain calm, and remarkably, some of the people in the front rows took their seats again. Even some of the people in the gallery sat back down. From the edge of the stage, Foy urged musical director Herbert Gillea to get some of the remaining musicians to play an overture, which had a temporary soothing effect on the crowd.

A few moments later, a flaming set crashed down onto the stage, and Foy asked everyone to get up and calmly leave the theatre. He told them to take their time, to not be frightened and to walk slowly as they exited. Then, he dropped his voice to a stagehand who was on the brink of fleeing from the theatre himself. "Lower that iron curtain! Drop the fire curtain!" he ordered. "For God's sake, does anyone know how this iron curtain is worked?"

Foy heard timbers cracking above his head, and he made one last entreaty that everyone proceed slowly from the theatre, but by now, no one was listening. As he looked out into the auditorium, he saw many of the people on the main floor leaving in an orderly fashion, but what he saw in the balcony and the gallery terrified him. In the upper tiers, he said, people were in a "mad, animal-like stampede."

Lester Linvonston, a young survivor who vividly recalled seeing Foy standing at the edge of the stage pleading for calm, was only distracted from the comedian by a macabre sight that appeared above Foy's head. "Almost alone and in the center of the house," Linvonston later said, he watched "a ballet dancer in a gauzy dress suspended by a steel belt from a wire. Her dress had caught fire and it burned like paper." The gruesome vision was Nellie Reed, the British star of the aerial ballet.

Finally, the asbestos curtain began to come down. Most of the stage crew had fled the theatre, but someone had figured out a way to lower what was thought would be a fireproof shield between the stage and the audience. It began inching its way down a steel cable between two wooden guide tracks. As if in slow motion, it descended, and then, less than twenty feet above the stage, it suddenly stopped. One end was jammed on the light reflector that had not been properly closed, and the other end sagged down to about five feet above the stage. The wooden guide tracks tore apart, and the curtain, which was supposed to have been reinforced and made stiff by steel rods and wires, began to billow out over the orchestra pit and the front rows of seats, pushed by the draft coming from an open stage exit that had been mobbed by the cast and crew.

Some stagehands tried to yank down the curtain, but it was no use. The rest of the crew ran for their lives. The theatre's engineer, Robert Murray, ran down to the basement and told his crew to shut off the steam in the boilers heating the building, bank all of the fires to prevent an explosion and then get out as fast as they could. Then he helped a group of chorus girls escape from a basement dressing room by pushing them, one at a time, through a coal chute that led to an alley. One or two of them were wearing street clothes, but the others were clad in their thin costumes or, worse, nothing but undergarments.

Murray rushed back up to the stage level and found a young woman whose costume and tights were shredded and burned and whose skin was charred and blistered. Nellie Reed had somehow unhooked herself from her wire but was seriously injured and in great pain. He managed to get her out into the street, where he handed her to some rescuers.

The entire stage had been turned into a blazing inferno, and if one of the stagehands had not opened one of the big double scenery doors, the entire cast might have perished. Opening the doors undoubtedly saved the lives of the cast and crew, but it sealed the fate of the audience in the upper tiers. The contractors who had built the theatre not only failed to connect the controls for the roof's ventilating systems but also nailed shut the vents over the stage and left open vents above the auditorium, creating a chimney effect. The blast of cold air that rushed in the scenery doors, causing the curtain to billow out from the stage, instantly mixed with the heated air fueled by the flames, and the result was a huge, deadly blowtorch that one fire official later described as a "back draft."

A churning column of smoke and flames burst out of the opening under the curtain, whirled above the orchestra pit and floor seats and swept into the balcony and gallery under the open roof vents like a fiery cyclone. The fireball sucked the oxygen from the air, burning and suffocating any in the upper tiers who remained in their seats or were trapped in the aisles.

Moments later, the last of the ropes holding up the scenery flats onstage gave away, and with a roar that literally shook the building, tons of wood, ropes, sandbags, pipes, pulleys, lights, rigging and more than 280 pieces of scenery crashed to the stage. The force of the fall instantly knocked out the electrical switchboard, and the auditorium was plunged into complete and utter darkness.

The aisles had become impassable, and as the lights went out, the crowd milled about in blind terror. The auditorium began to fill with heat and smoke, and screams echoed off the walls and ceilings. Many of those who died not only burned but also suffocated from the smoke and the crush of bodies. Later, as the police removed the charred remains from the theatre, they discovered that a number of victims had been trampled in the panic. One dead woman's face even bore the mark of a shoe heel. Mothers and children were wrenched away from one another and trampled by those behind them. Dresses, jackets, trousers and other articles of clothing were ripped to shreds as people tried to get through to the exits and escape the flames and smoke. When the crowd reached the doors, it could not open them as they had been designed to swing inward rather than outward. The crush of people prevented those in the front from opening the doors. To make matters worse, some of the side doors to the auditorium were reportedly locked.

In desperation, some of those whose clothing had caught fire jumped from the first balcony to the floor below. Many of them died instantly. Others suffered agonizing deaths from broken backs caused by landing on armrests and seat backs.

A brief rush of light illuminated the hellish scene as the safety curtain burst into flames. The curtain, it turned out, was not made completely from asbestos but from some cheaper material that had been chosen by the theatre's co-owner, Will Davis.

At that moment, Eddie Foy made a fateful decision. He needed to get out of the theatre as quickly as possible and first considered following the crowd through the Randolph Street doors. But wanting to find his son, he changed his mind and made his way through the burning backstage and out the scenery doors. He would only realize how lucky his decision had been after he learned of the hundreds of victims found crushed inside those Randolph Street doors.

Inside the theatre, the badly burned house fireman, William Sallers, was shoving members of the cast and crew out of the scenery doors and into the alley. By now, Engine 13 should have arrived, and he stepped outside and began shouting for the commander, Captain Jennings. Sallers believed that if he could get the fire crew through the scenery doors and onto the stage, it could prevent the blaze from reaching the audience. But when he looked behind him, he saw flames roaring out the doors. He later recalled, "I knew that anybody who was in there was gone. I knew there was no chance to get out."

In the time that had been lost because the Iroquois had no alarm system, the theatre had turned into an oven. When collecting valuables after the fire, the police found at least a dozen watches that had been stopped at about the same time, 3:50 p.m. This meant that nearly twenty minutes had elapsed from the time that the first alarm had been raised. This certainly accounted for the jamming at the exits and the relatively few people eyewitnesses saw leaving the theatre. Some of the witnesses later stated that nearly seven minutes passed from the time they saw fire coming from the roof of the theatre to the front doors on Randolph Street being opened.

Strangely, when Engine 13 arrived at the Randolph Street doors, the scene outside of the theatre was completely normal. If not for the smoke billowing from the roof, the firefighters would have assumed that it was a false alarm. This changed when they tried to open the auditorium doors and found that they could not—there were too many bodies stacked up against them. They were only able to gain access by actually pulling the bodies out of the way with pike poles, peeling them off one another and then climbing over the stacks of corpses. It took only ten minutes to put out the remaining blaze, as the intense heat inside had already eaten up anything that would still burn.

The gallery and upper balcony sustained the greatest loss of life because the patrons who had been seated there were trapped by locked doors and gates at the top of the stairways. The firefighters found two hundred bodies stacked there, as many as ten deep.

A few who made it to the fire escape door behind the top balcony found that the iron staircase was missing. In its place was a platform that plunged about fifty feet into Couch Place, a cobblestone alley below. Across the alley, behind the theatre, painters were working on a building occupied by Northwestern University's dental school. When they realized what was happening at the theatre, they quickly erected a makeshift bridge using a ladder, which they extended across the alley to the fire escape platform. Several people made it to safety, but then, as another man was edging his way across, the ladder slipped off the icy ledge of the university building, and the man plummeted to his death.

After the ladder was lost, three wide boards were pushed across to the theatre, and the painters anchored them with their knees. The plank bridge worked for a time, but it could not handle the crush of people spilling out of the theatre exit. The painters helped as many people as they could, but when what sounded like a bomb went off in the theatre (the sound of the rigging and scenery falling to the stage), they watched helplessly as the people trapped inside tried in vain to escape.

Those who swarmed from the fire escape exit were pushed to the edge of the railings with nowhere to go. It was impossible for them to turn back because of the crowd behind them, and they were pushed over the side. Some people tried to crawl across the planks, but in the confusion and smoke, they slipped and fell to the alley. Others, whose clothing was on fire, simply gave up and jumped from the railings.

The boards began falling away, and as the fire grew, flames shot out the doors and windows along the theatre's wall. Many of those hoping for rescue were burned alive in full view of the painters and students at the dental school. From some of Northwestern University's windows, onlookers could see directly into the theatre, which was a solid mass of flames. In the middle of the inferno, they could see men, women and children running about, and students later said that they did not even look human.

In the aftermath of the fire, Couch Place was dubbed "Death Alley" by reporters who arrived on the scene and counted nearly 150 victims lying on the slush-covered cobblestones. The bodies had been stacked there by firemen or had fallen from above.

For nearly five hours, police officers, firemen and even newspaper reporters carried out the dead. Anxious relatives sifted through the ruins, searching for loved ones. As the news spread, public response

The burned-out seats in front of the stage at the Iroquois Theatre.

Firefighters at work in Couch Place, the passageway behind the Iroquois Theater that reporters soon dubbed "Death Alley" because of the corpses that were stacked there after the fire.

was immediate and overwhelming. A nearby medical school sent one hundred students to help the doctors who had been dispatched to the Iroquois. A hardware company down the street emptied its stock of two hundred lanterns. Marshall Field's; Mandel Brothers; Carson, Pirie, Scott; and other department stores sent piles of blankets, sheets, rolls of linen, packages of cotton and large delivery wagons and converted their ground-floor restrooms and lounges into emergency medical stations. Montgomery Ward sent one of its new, large motorized delivery wagons, but even with its bell ringing, it could not get through the crowds that were jammed into the streets and had to turn back. Other bodies were taken away by police wagons and ambulances and transported to a temporary morgue at Marshall Field's on State Street. Medical examiners and investigators worked through the night.

Within a short time, small restaurants, saloons and stores in the vicinity of the Iroquois had been turned into improvised aid stations as medical workers and volunteers began arriving in large numbers. Chicago's central telephone exchange was overwhelmed by emergency calls.

Because the hardware store lanterns were not powerful enough to illuminate the blackened auditorium, the Edison Company rushed over forty arc lamps, and when they were turned on, fire and rescue workers were stunned by what they saw. Some of the audience had died sitting in their seats, facing the stage. Others had no burn marks or bruises on them because they had suffocated quickly from the smoke. Many women were found with their heads resting on the back of the seat in front of them. A young boy's head was missing. One woman was bent back over the seat she had been sitting in, her spine severed. Hundreds had been trampled. Clothing, shoes, pocketbooks and other personal belongings were strewn about. Some of the bodies were burned beyond recognition.

Scores of victims had been wedged into doorways. A husband and wife were locked so tightly in one another's arms that they had to be removed from the theatre together. A mother had thrown her arms around her daughter in a hopeless effort to save her, and both had been burned beyond recognition. The number of dead children was heartbreaking. Many were found burned; others had been trampled. Two dead children were found with the kneeling body of their mother, who had tried to shield them from the flames.

At the edge of the auditorium, a fireman emerged from the ashes with the body of a little girl in his arms. He groped his way forward, stumbling toward Fire Marshal William Henry Musham, who ordered him to give the child to someone else and get back into the auditorium. As the fireman came closer, the marshal and the other officers could see the streaks of tears on the man's soot-covered face. "I'm sorry, chief," the man said, "but I've got a little one like this at home. I want to carry this one out." The weeping fireman carried the little body down the steps of what only an hour before had been the glittering promenade of the grandest theatre in Chicago.

With the aid of the Edison arc lights, Deputy Fire Chief John Campion searched the theatre's interior while his men continued to douse hot spots that occasionally still burst into flames. Campion called out for survivors, looking around at the burned seats, the blackened walls and the twisted piles of debris that littered the stage.

The devastated Iroquois theatre was silent.

In less than a quarter of an hour, 572 lives had ended in the Iroquois Theatre. More died later, bringing the death toll up to 602, including 212 children. Hundreds more had been injured in what was supposed to be the safest theatre in the city. The number of dead was greater than those who had perished in the Great Fire of 1871.

The next day, the newspapers devoted full pages to lists of the known dead and injured. News wires carried reports of the tragedy around the country, and it soon became a national disaster. Chicago mayor Carter Harrison Jr. issued an order that banned public celebration on New Year's Eve, closing the nightclubs and forbidding any fireworks or sounding of horns. Every church and factory bell in the city was silenced, and on January 2, 1904, the city observed an official day of mourning.

Someone, the public cried, had to answer for the fire, and an investigation of the blaze brought to light a number of troubling facts, including the faulty vents and the fact that one of them had been nailed shut. Another finding showed that the supposedly "fireproof" asbestos curtain was really made from cotton and other combustible materials. It wouldn't have saved anyone at all. In addition to not having any fire alarms in the building, the owners had decided that sprinklers were too unsightly and costly and had never had them installed.

News reports revealed management's policy to keep nonpaying customers from slipping into the theatre during a performance—quietly bolting nine pairs of iron panels over the rear doors and installing padlocked, accordion-style gates at the top of the interior second- and third-floor stairway landings. Equally as tragic was the idea it came up with to keep the audience from being distracted during a show—ordering all of the exit lights to be turned off. One exit sign that was left on led

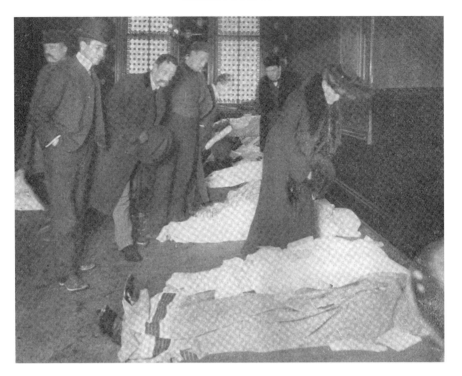

Parents search through the bodies of the dead from the Iroquois Theatre, looking for their children.

to ladies' restroom and another to a locked door for a private stairway. And as mentioned previously, the doors of the outside exits, which were supposed to make it possible for the theatre to empty in five minutes, opened to the inside, not the outside.

The investigation led to a coverup by officials from the city and the fire department, which denied all knowledge of fire code violations. They blamed the inspectors, who had overlooked the problems in exchange for free theatre passes. A grand jury indicted a number of individuals, including the theatre owners, fire officials and even the mayor. No one was ever charged with a criminal act, however. Families of the dead filed nearly 275 civil lawsuits against the theatre, but no money was ever collected. The Iroquois Theatre Company filed for bankruptcy soon after the disaster.

Nevertheless, the building was repaired and reopened briefly in 1904 as Hyde and Behmann's Music Hall and later, in 1905, as the Colonial Theatre. In 1924, the building was razed to make room for a new theatre, the Oriental, but the façade of the Iroquois was used in its construction. The Oriental operated at what is now 24 West Randolph Street until the middle part of 1981, when it fell into disrepair and was closed down. It opened again as the home to a wholesale electronics dealer for a time and then went dark again. The restored theatre is now part of the Civic Tower Building next door to the restored Delaware Building. It reopened as the Ford Center for the Performing Arts in 1998.

Tragically, there is not a single marker or plaque dedicated to the hundreds of victims who perished in the blaze. There was a plaque unveiled by politicians and city leaders in 2003, the 100th anniversary of the fire, but it has never been installed at the theatre, in Couch Place or anywhere else.

The controversy over the fire may have faded away many years ago, but the lessons learned from it should never be forgotten. The Iroquois Theatre Fire ranks as the nation's fourth deadliest blaze and the deadliest single-building fire in American history. It remains one of Chicago's worst tragedies and is a chilling reminder of how the past continues to reverberate into the present.

CHICAGO'S FIRST "ONE-WAY RIDE"

Although the gangland "one-way ride" didn't become a slang term for an underworld execution method until the Prohibition era, the first such ride in Chicago actually predated the Volstead Act by more than a decade and a half. The usual plan was for the victim, who was lured or forced into a car, to be driven to a remote location where he would be killed and his body dumped.

The term for this type of execution was reportedly first used by North Side gang member Hymie Weiss, who was the last person to be seen in the company of Steve Wisniewski, a local criminal who had recently hijacked a North Side beer shipment in July 1921. When he returned, Weiss explained the man's disappearance by saying that he "took Stevie for a one-way ride."

This method was used countless times in gangland executions of the era, and bodies of rival mobsters were often found in remote locations throughout the Chicago area during the 1920s and 1930s. However, the very first "one-way ride" actually took place on November 18, 1904, when a dashing ladies' man named John William "Billy" Bate was last seen in a car traveling south on Michigan Avenue with his killer at his side.

About 9:15 p.m. that evening, Billy Bate was seen in a mint green Pope-Toledo touring car traveling south on Michigan Avenue near Congress. Wearing a chauffer's cap, goggles and driving gloves,

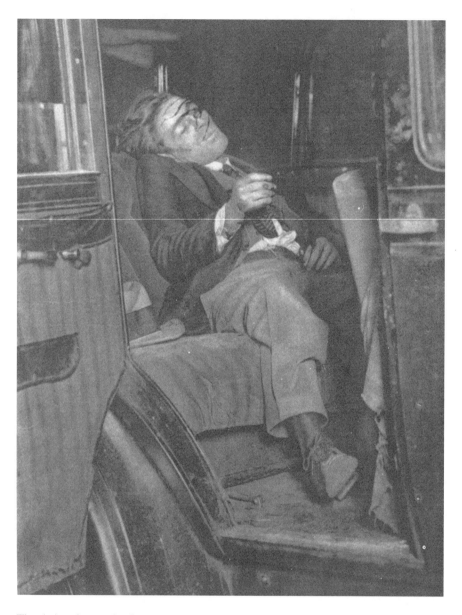

The victim of a gangland "one-way ride."

he was chatting with his passenger, a man who had introduced himself as Mr. Dove. This name was overheard by Edward Slavin, a telephone operator at the Auditorium Hotel, and Chicago police detectives carefully took note.

On the morning of November 19, a farmer named Peter Freehauf found the touring car parked along an abandoned road near his home in south suburban Lemont. Billy Bate was slumped over the steering wheel. He had been shot twice in the back of the head with a .22-caliber pistol.

Who had killed the young man—and why?

As the police began to investigate the crime, they discovered the mysterious figure of Mr. Dove, as well as Bate's string of jilted girlfriends, which ultimately led to his death.

On the previous evening, Mr. Dove had approached the registration desk of the Auditorium Hotel and had asked the switchboard operator to telephone the Wabash Avenue garage for a car and driver. He needed a vehicle that would accommodate two passengers, he said, and after some bargaining, he agreed to pay the driver five dollars an hour. The operator placed a call to Dan Canary's garage, where Billy Bate was passing the time with some other drivers in a game of coin toss.

Bate agreed to take the call and asked the night manager if Dove was "all right." Edwin Archer, who had taken the call but later remembered nothing more about it than the fact that the customer had argued about the price, told Bate, "I don't know, and I don't care. Get your money and pick him up."

Witnesses later described Mr. Dove as a wealthy-looking man who was attired in evening clothes and a derby hat. A bystander claimed that he heard Dove exchange some heated words with Bate as the car pulled away from the curb, but aside from that, no evidence about the man existed.

The police learned that another witness, a farmhand on his way home from a date, had seen the touring car later that night, about midnight. It was parked on Archer Avenue, about three miles outside of Lemont. The farmhand said that he saw three people in the automobile, and one of them was a woman. Peter Freehauf, the man who reported Bate's body the next morning, said that he and his wife had heard someone pounding on their door during the early morning hours, followed by two gunshots in rapid succession. The couple huddled in terror, refusing to open the door. At dawn, they ventured outside and found Bate behind the wheel of his car. He had been shot in the back of the head on the muddy, deserted road.

Detectives were able to trace some of Dove's movements. He continued to Joliet by train, wagon or some other method, pausing at a boardinghouse to purchase a bottle of benzene (a harsh cleaning solution) to get some of the blood out of his clothes. A kitchen helper at the house described Dove as a nervous chain smoker who smelled of women's perfume. The helper also noted that his teeth were very small and white and that he had a soft voice "like a woman." He apparently confessed to having a girlfriend in Pittsburgh, an admission that the police found interesting since Bate claimed to have a fiancée there. The police entertained the idea that the chauffer had been murdered by a woman posing as a man but eventually concluded that Dove was a man, albeit an effeminate one.

Mr. Dove boarded a train in Joliet the next day and was never seen again.

The police pulled five love letters from the dead man's vest pocket, and the next day, the *Chicago American* printed allegations that Bate was keeping company with a wealthy society matron and had left a trail of broken hearts and spurned lovers that extended from New York to Chicago. One of the more poignant letters was from a woman named Rose, who wrote:

> *I understand you have won the love of Bertha, and I presume that you have no further use for me. I hope that your future love will be successful. Of course it is pretty hard on me, but I will let the matter drop and say no more. With love, Rose*

Investigators scoured the countryside looking for clues about the identity of the woman who was seen in Bate's car. They even searched for a body, in case she had been murdered too. One theory held that Mr. Dove had forced Bate to pick up the woman outside of Chicago, murdered the woman and then turned the weapon on Bate. The nearby canal and the roadside ditches were searched, but the woman was never found. If a woman had been murdered in the midst of this drama, the killer had caused her to vanish without a trace.

The Bate murder mystery, although mostly forgotten today, was the subject of newspaper stories and gossip for many weeks to come. A female detective (very rare in those days) was brought into the case to look over the facts and draw her own conclusions, but there was little for her to examine. The investigation foundered and then went cold. It was suggested by some that the murder was the desperate act of a scorned lover or part of a conspiracy that had been hatched by the elusive Mr. Dove. Or perhaps Bate was nothing more than a small-time hood who fell in with the wrong people and ended up in the wrong place at the wrong time.

We will never know for sure, but Billy Bate earned a place in the history of Chicago crime as the victim of the city's first "one-way ride."

"THERE'S A SUCKER BORN EVERY MINUTE!"

Although most people today don't remember Mike McDonald, the Chicago gambler and political boss of the 1880s, he contributed three phrases to the Windy City lexicon that are still recalled today. In 1873, McDonald built a huge, four-story gambling establishment, called the Store, that took up nearly a square block. Just before it opened, his partner asked him if he thought the place was too large, and McDonald answered, "Don't worry about that. There's a sucker born every minute." Legend has it that McDonald was also the first man to utter the phrase, "Never give a sucker an even break."

He was also responsible for a quip that became a staple of vaudeville shows of the era. McDonald loathed the police. One day, a man came to him and asked him for two dollars, and McDonald asked what it was for. The man replied that he and some others were burying a policeman. "Fine," McDonald answered, "Here's ten dollars. Bury five of them."

But Mike McDonald was not just a man who went about Chicago saying clever things. When he arrived in the city at the age of fifteen, he was already an accomplished card dealer and made his way by selling half-empty boxes of candy on trains. During the Civil War, he had another racket—enlisting in the army. There were bounties paid for enlistments, and McDonald worked it out so that he would get a commission from every one of his men he got to join up. The

Mike McDonald (right), the first king of organized crime in Chicago. *Courtesy of the* Chicago Daily News.

men would enlist, desert and enlist again, gaining commissions for the boss and putting money in their own pockets.

One of McDonald's gambling establishments burned in the Great Fire in 1871, but he was able to rebuild quickly. The gambling parlor went up right next to the brothels and gin joints, which legend claims were among the first structures to return after the disaster. His profits from a single gambling parlor on the west side were said to be over $100,000 a year. In Chicago, a man with that sort of money went into politics, which was exactly what McDonald did.

McDonald backed Harvey D. Colvin, a gambler who was also the general agent of the United States Express Co., for the mayor's office. Colvin ran as a "law and order" candidate, which is ironic considering the company he kept. During his wide-open administration, David Kalakua, the king of the Hawaiian Islands, visited Chicago. Colvin spent most of the day trying to communicate with the king in sign language and wild gestures before learning that Kalakua spoke fluent English.

By the end of Colvin's term in office, there were two mayors of Chicago, thanks to an incredible legal blunder. The mayoral election had been changed from fall to spring, and the city council passed an ordinance calling for the election of city officers but never mentioned the office of mayor. The council tried to rectify the situation, but the motion for a special mayoral election was defeated. Colvin then claimed that since no election had been officially called, he could stay in office—which he did. However, this didn't stop others from holding the election. A meeting was held, and Thomas Hoyne was nominated. He was "elected" on April 18, 1876, but Colvin refused to step down, despite the fact that Hoyne was in an office at city hall demanding to be recognized as the mayor. Eventually, the circuit court ruled that Colvin was Chicago's only mayor, even though the city council had already recognized Hoyne as its presiding officer.

Meanwhile, Mike McDonald was reaping a fortune off the "suckers" who came into the Store, as well as his other establishments. In those days, he literally ran the criminal element of Chicago, taking a tariff on everything that was stolen, on all gambling proceeds and on all profits from prostitution and blackmail schemes. His control over the city was absolute. Twice each year, phony police raids were carried out on the Store (with McDonald's permission, of course) so that the newspapers could have their headlines. Those who crossed McDonald, even the cops, had to answer for it. For instance, in 1880, the Store was subjected to an unscheduled raid by Police Superintendent Simon O'Donnell. For his efforts, O'Donnell was demoted to a captain's position and given the worst assignments for the rest of his years on the force.

The Store became a gathering place for some of the most celebrated criminals of the era. Herbert Asbury wrote that if you stayed in the boardinghouse that McDonald's wife ran on an upper floor, you might meet Hungry Joe Lewis, who took Oscar Wilde for several thousand dollars in a card game; Red Jimmy Fitzgerald, a swindler who made off with $7,000 that belonged to a famous diplomat; McDonald's one-armed brother-in-law, Nick Hogan, who, "if he had both arms," one policeman claimed, would "have all of money in the world"; and Tom O'Brien, Chicago's most celebrated bunco man until he went to Paris in 1895 and murdered Reed Waddell, the inventor of the goldbrick fraud. During the World's Fair in 1893, O'Brien and several others made $500,000 in five months.

The most active of McDonald's crooks was Hank Davis, a faro dealer, forger, thief, con man and leader of a gang that included

Billy Brush, Ross Saulsbury and Jim Fay. If a woman was needed to carry out a job, Davis used Saulsbury's wife, an educated woman who graduated from college and who was the daughter of a New York clergyman. She had also been a prostitute and a brothel inmate when Saulsbury married her. During a trip to Pennsylvania, Saulsbury was arrested and sent to prison, and his wife immediately went to live with Davis. She accompanied Davis on a trip to the South in the fall of 1875, and when they returned to Chicago, Davis went on a drinking binge. On November 25, falling down drunk, he called on his friend Charles Whyland, the owner of the St. Elmo Saloon and Restaurant on South Dearborn Street, and invited Whyland and his wife to dinner. The saloonkeeper stated that he and his wife were not interested in being seen with Davis socially, whereupon Davis pulled out a revolver and shot Whyland three times. Whyland died an hour later. When he was told that he might hang for the murder, Davis replied, "It was an unfortunate scrape and I can't blame anything but drink." Instead of being hanged, however, Davis was sent to Joliet Penitentiary for twenty-one years.

The boardinghouse on the upper floors of the Store was the exclusive enterprise of McDonald's wife, Mrs. Mary Noonan McDonald, whose hatred of the police, at least during the early years of their marriage, was almost as intense as her husband's. The policemen who carried out the phone raids on the Store were under strict orders not to go above the second floor, but Mary occasionally had problems with overly diligent officers who insisted on searching the rooms of her guests. In November 1878, when several policemen blundered into her kitchen and began peering into her cupboards, she became so enraged that she fired a pistol at them and struck one of the patrolmen in the arm. She was arrested, but thanks to McDonald's influence and the legal skills of A.S. Trude, a famous criminal lawyer who often represented McDonald's cronies, she was discharged on the grounds that she was merely defending her home from invasion. McDonald's saloon license was ceremoniously revoked, but it was restored a week later.

McDonald made a fortune with the Store, but perhaps his greatest scheme was when he swindled the City of Chicago. He managed to get the city and the county to award him a contract to paint the courthouse with a "secret preserving fluid." The bill for the job was $128,250, and half of the money was paid out before the *Chicago*

Daily News discovered that the secret fluid was only chalk and water. McDonald was never prosecuted for the scam.

Despite his decades in gambling, politics and as an underworld boss, his career stumbled in the late 1880s. In 1887, an honest mayor, John A. Roche, took over office and forced McDonald out of business. Roche told the gamblers and confidence men that he planned to close them down and soon proved by repeated raids and arrests that he meant what he said. They left the city in droves, and McDonald went looking for another line of work. Always the opportunist, he severed his connections with the con men and bunco artists and sublet his wife's boardinghouse to a Mrs. Ross, who had been in business at that same location before the Great Fire as "the only scientific astrologer in the west." He turned over the control of the Store to Parson Davies, a well-known sporting man.

McDonald took the more than $2 million that he had saved and decided to try to make an honest living. He purchased a newspaper, the *Chicago Globe*, and ran it for two years. He also helped to build the city's first elevated railway and sold stone and gravel from a quarry in Lemont to city contracts.

McDonald built a magnificent home on Ashland Avenue, near the residence of his friend and Chicago mayor Carter Harrison. He lived there with his wife and two children. They had been living in the mansion for only two months when Mary McDonald disappeared. She eloped with an actor named Billy Anderson, a minstrel singer who had come to Chicago as a member of the Emerson troupe. The gambler followed after them and finally brought her back from San Francisco, where she was living with Arlington at the Palace Hotel.

The couple reconciled, and then, in 1889, she left again, this time with the Reverend Joseph Moysant, assistant rector of the Catholic Church of Notre Dame. After living in Paris for several years, the priest entered a monastery, and Mrs. McDonald returned to Chicago, where she opened a boardinghouse.

Meanwhile, not long after his wife absconded with the priest, McDonald renounced Catholicism and obtained a divorce. A short time later, he married Dora Feldman, who was twenty-three years old and a former playmate of the McDonald children. McDonald was forty-nine at the time. He built a mansion for Dora on Drexel Boulevard, and they lived happily together—or so it seemed—until February 1907.

In the early days of that year, Dora had strayed into the arms of a teenage boy named Webster Guerin, a young commercial artist. The violently passionate affair ended in murder when Dora stormed into Guerin's office in a fit of rage one morning in February and shot the young man in the neck. She told the police that Guerin had been her lover, and she talked freely of her affection for him and her loathing of McDonald.

McDonald never recovered from the shock of the killing or his wife's confessions, and his health was ruined. He spent several months in the hospital and then died on August 9, 1907.

Although McDonald allegedly embraced the Catholic Church again on his deathbed and stated that Mary was his only true wife, she received nothing from his estate. Dora received one-third of it, plus $40,000 for her murder defense fund. She was acquitted of the Guerin shooting in 1908.

Chicago's "Bluebeard"

In order to try and adequately understand the life and crimes of a man who was known by various names, including Johann Otto Hoch, we have to begin by looking at the end of his criminal career rather than the beginning. It was not until the investigation that was started by Chicago police inspector George Shippy that the extent of Hoch's crimes was discovered. Thanks to Shippy's tedious and detailed investigation into the murky past of the killer, the inspector came to believe that scores of false names and identities concealed the presence of a single murderer—a man who had taken the lives of at least a dozen women. It was after an arrest for swindling that Shippy was able to reveal a devious criminal who was at that time unequaled in the annals of American homicide.

Johann Otto Hoch, who married and murdered for nineteen years before his capture, was born John Schmidt in Horweiler, Germany, in 1862. He was married for the first time to a woman named Christine Ramb before deserting her and their three children in 1887. While investigating a charge of bigamy and another charge of swindling a furniture dealer, Inspector Shippy first came into contact with Hoch in 1898. At that time, Hoch was using the alias of Martin Dotz.

The inspector had no way of knowing that Hoch/Dotz had murdered a dozen women all over the country, but he became suspicious when he received a letter from Reverend Herman Haas of

Johann Otto Hoch (lower left), the Chicago Bluebeard who may have slain as many as fifty women, at the time of his trial in 1905. *Courtesy of the Chicago Historical Society.*

Wheeling, West Virginia. Haas had recognized Hoch's photograph in a Chicago newspaper, and he sent the police a photograph of the man who was suspected of killing Mrs. Caroline Hoch in the summer of 1895. There was no mistaking the fact that the man in the photo and the man in the police station holding cell were the same person. The problem was that the man in the photograph was supposed to have committed suicide by drowning himself in the Ohio River three years before.

Shippy attempted to pursue this lead but realized that it was going to take a lot of time. He needed to keep Hoch in jail, so he turned his efforts to the swindling charge. He soon had enough for a conviction, and Hoch was sentenced to a year in the Cook County jail. Shippy then turned his attention back to Hoch's other illegal activities and, acting on a tip, began to search for what became a dozen missing wives. He started in West Virginia.

Hoch first appeared in Wheeling in February 1895, going by the name Jacob Huff. He opened a saloon in a German neighborhood and became a popular man in the community. He began to seek out marriageable widows or at least divorced women with money. One of those he found was Caroline Hoch, a middle-aged widow. The couple married in April, and the service was performed by Reverend Haas. It was the minister who discovered Caroline dying in agony after he spotted her husband giving her some sort of white powder. The reverend did not act, however, believing that it was merely medicine, but the woman died a few days later in great pain. Huff (as he was known) insisted that his wife be buried right away. He then collected Caroline's life insurance, sold her house, cleaned out her bank accounts and disappeared.

Reverend Haas later explained to Inspector Shippy what he believed happened next. Huff strolled to the nearby Ohio River on the night of his disappearance, stripped off his clothes and walked into the water. He placed his good watch, with his photo in the locket, and a suicide note on the pile of clothing and then, holding a heavy sack over his head, walked into the river to a rowboat. He climbed into the boat, which he had earlier anchored, and dressed in the clothing that he had hidden there. Afterward, he rowed up the river, only pausing in the deep water to drop the bag that he had carefully carried with him. He continued on to the Ohio side of the river, set the boat adrift and then resumed his journey. He was no longer Jacob Huff but Johann Otto Hoch, taking the last name of his victim. To investigators, it appeared that Huff had committed suicide.

For almost a year, Shippy followed Hoch's strange trail across the country, and he found scores of dead and deserted women, from New York to San Francisco, with most of the victims being in the Midwest. Years later, he would unearth even more—perhaps as many as fifty—in St. Louis, Minneapolis, Kansas City, Philadelphia and beyond. Inspector Shippy was stunned by what he discovered. Hoch was not an attractive man. He was short, fat and wheezy and had a German accent that was so pronounced that it was sometimes difficult to understand what he was saying. And yet, somehow, this unappealing little man seduced and married countless widows and lonely old spinsters.

Incredibly, despite his thorough investigations, Shippy could not produce enough hard evidence to convict Hoch of anything, and the man was soon due to be released from jail. Desperately, Shippy contacted the authorities in Wheeling and begged them to exhume the body of Caroline Hoch to look for signs of arsenic poisoning.

The request was carried out, and the coffin was exhumed from the cemetery. However, officials were stunned when the lid was opened and it was discovered that all of the cadaver's vital organs had been surgically removed. It was later decided that this must have been what was in the weighted bag that Hoch had carried with him and then dumped in the middle of the river. The body could not be examined, which meant that there was no real case to be made against Hoch for Caroline's murder. At the end of his term for swindling, Hoch was released, much to the dismay of Inspector Shippy. He was convinced that the man would murder again.

From 1900 to 1904, Hoch, using various aliases and married and murdered as many as fifteen more women. Prior to his prison term in Chicago for swindling, Hoch married women and then slowly poisoned them to death, calling in doctors whom he knew would innocently diagnose his wife's ailment as a disease of the kidneys, for which there was no treatment. He took his time, spending months murdering his wives very carefully. After his release from the Cook County jail, however, Hoch's careful method fell to pieces. He began killing in record time, marrying rich widows and, within days of the wedding, heavily dosing them with arsenic. He murdered some of his wives within a week of their nuptials. He married his last victim, Marie Walcker, in Chicago on December 5, 1904, and he poisoned her only a few days later.

On the night of Marie's death, the victim's estranged sister, Amelia, appeared at her home. As his wife lay dying, Hoch embraced and kissed Amelia and asked her to marry him after the death of her sister. Amazingly, she agreed. Marie was buried a day later, without being embalmed, and Hoch married Amelia six days after the service. The killer had received $500 from Marie's life insurance policy, and Amelia gave him another $750. He disappeared immediately afterward, and Amelia went to the Chicago police. Inspector Shippy had Marie Walcker's body exhumed, and poison was found in her organs. The search was now on for the killer.

Shippy sent photographs of Hoch to every major newspaper in the country, and a short time later, a widowed landlady in New York, Mrs. Katherine Kimmerle, recognized the likeness as being that of her new boarder, Henry Bartels. She recalled him so vividly because the strange man had proposed marriage to her only twenty minutes after he had taken the room. The authorities soon had Hoch in custody.

When he was arrested, Hoch claimed that he was being framed and that the "truth" about him was misrepresented. Discovered in his room were $625, several wedding rings with the inscriptions filed off, a loaded revolver and a fountain pen that contained fifty-eight grams of arsenic. Hoch claimed that he had planned to commit suicide with the poison. He was soon on his way back to Chicago. Inspector Shippy was waiting for him when the train arrived in the station.

During his trial, the killer hummed, whistled and twirled his thumbs in court. His demeanor shocked the public and the court officials because he seemed so content and happy to be there. Perhaps more shocking, however, was his treatment in his jail cell. He was given comfortable couches, books and newspapers, Porterhouse steaks and beer. This was a far cry from the beans and black coffee that were given to most prisoners. He was often allowed to take walks, during which he flirted with and ogled every woman he saw. Hoch received scores of marriage proposals and comic valentines, which he delighted in reading. Police officials stated that Hoch paid for his treatment in jail—or at least he bribed the right people.

Until the very end, Hoch insisted that he was innocent. When he was finally convicted of murdering Marie Walcker, Hoch only whispered, "It's all over with Johann. It serves me right." He clung to the hope that he would be released until the very hour of his death. He remained awake all night before the day of the execution, eating huge meals and demanding more and more food. Every now and then, he would smile at his guards and say, "Look at me, boys. Look at poor old Johann. I don't look like a monster now, do I?" The guards did not reply.

Legal appeals were funded by various groups that tried to save Hoch. On the day before his scheduled hanging, Hoch needed $600 to launch an appeal with the Illinois Supreme Court. The gallows had already been built, but a stranger came forward with the money. The appeal was denied, only postponing his death a little while longer.

Strangely, Amelia Walcker, the woman who had turned him in, eventually took his side. She visited his cell daily, mended his clothes and begged for his forgiveness. Many believed that she might have had a hand in her sister's death, assisting her killer out of jealousy. The strange way that she behaved toward Hoch led many to speculate.

Even the officials at the jail were sympathetic toward Hoch. His seductive manner seemed to have almost cast a spell over them. On the day that he was to be hanged, the assistant jailer refused to lead Hoch to the gallows, and someone else had to be found to do the job.

Meanwhile, in an exclusive for the *Chicago Sun*, Hoch revealed his six secrets for seducing women:

1. Nine out of every ten women can be won by flattery.

2. Never let a woman know her own shortcomings.

3. Always appear to a woman to be the anxious one.

4. Women like to be told pleasant things about themselves.

5. When you make love, be ardent and earnest.

6. The average man can fool the average woman if he will only let her have her own way at the start.

Hoch finally went to the gallows on February 23, 1906. He once more declared his innocence and then nodded for the sheriff to place the noose around his neck. He declared, "I am done with this world. I have done with everybody." Moments later, the trap was sprung, and Johann Hoch went to his death, bringing an end to one of the most depraved murder careers in American history.

MURDER IN A FLOWER SHOP

THE ASSASSINATION OF DION O'BANION

In the spring of 1924, Johnny Torrio and Al Capone were the reigning kings of the Chicago underworld, but trouble was coming, and most of it was being caused by Dion O'Banion.

Dean Charles O'Banion was born in 1892 in the small central Illinois town of Maroa. His father, Charles, was a barber by trade who hailed from Lincoln, Illinois, and his mother, the former Emma Brophy, was the Chicago-born daughter of an Irish immigrant father and American mother. She was just eight months old when the Great Chicago Fire leveled the city in 1871. Charles and Emma married in 1886, and the following year they moved to Maroa, where Charles's parents lived.

Dean spent the early years of his life in Maroa, but soon after the birth of his sister, Ruth, his mother contracted tuberculosis and died in 1901. Dean was only nine years old at the time, and the loss was devastating to him and his remaining family. They packed up and moved to Chicago, where Emma's parents had a place for them. Dean (soon to be known as Dion) saw the end of his innocent years. The hard times, and the legend, were about to begin.

Upon moving to Chicago, O'Banion found himself turning to the streets for a playground. He became involved with a street gang known as the Little Hellions and began picking pockets and rolling drunks. At the same time, he sang in the choir at the Holy Name Cathedral, and on Sundays, he served as an altar boy. Some of the priests at the church believed that his devotion might lead to the priesthood, but O'Banion soon learned to ration his religion to Sundays and to devote his remaining time to robbery and, as he reached young adulthood, burglary: "a man's profession."

For a time, O'Banion worked as a singing waiter at the McGovern brother's café and saloon on North Clark Street, crooning and balancing a hefty tray of beer glasses. McGovern's was a rough place filled with crooks. It was here that O'Banion met, and befriended, notorious safecrackers and thieves like George "Bugs" Moran, Earl "Hymie" Weiss, Vincent "the Schemer" Drucci and Samuel "Nails" Morton. With these men at his side, O'Banion put together one of the most devastating gangs in Chicago. They centered their activities on the North Side, around Lincoln Park and the Gold Coast.

O'Banion earned a reputation as a daring, ambidextrous, flower-loving, good-natured killer who wore a carnation in his buttonhole and carried three pistols stowed away in special pockets that had been sewn into his suits by his tailors. Chief of Police Morgan Collins called O'Banion "Chicago's arch criminal" and declared that he had killed, or ordered killed, at least twenty-five men. But

Dion O'Banion, the leader of the mob on the North Side of Chicago. He was a constant source of trouble for Johnny Torrio and Al Capone, who controlled the Chicago syndicate. *Courtesy of the* Chicago Daily News.

he was never brought to trial for any of these murders because, politically speaking, he was only slightly less powerful than Torrio and Capone. He was particularly powerful in the Forty-second and Forty-third Wards on the North Side, and for years, he and his gunmen kept these areas Democratic. So widely was his ability as a vote getter recognized that a quip went around, saying, "Who'll carry the Forty-second and Forty-third Wards? O'Banion, in his pistol pocket."

As the November 1924 election approached, disturbing rumors circulated among Democratic politicians that O'Banion was considering throwing in with the Republicans. To avert such a calamity, a dinner was held in O'Banion's honor at the Webster Hotel in Lincoln Park, at which the gangster was presented with a platinum watch encrusted with diamonds and rubies. The sponsor of the dinner, and the purchaser of the watch, was never revealed. Among the guests were Frank Gusenberg; Vincent Drucci; George Moran; Hymie Weiss; Louis Alterie, who besides being a gunmen for O'Banion was also the president of the Theater and Buildings Janitors' Union; Jerry O'Connor, a gambling house owner and the vice-president of the union; and Con Shea, a notorious labor slugger and racketeer who had served a term in Sing Sing for the attempted murder of a woman. These colorful mobsters were joined at the dinner by Colonel Albert A. Sprague, Chicago's commissioner of public works and Democratic candidate for U.S. senator; County Clerk Robert Sweitzer; Chief of Detectives Michael Hughes; and a half dozen police captains and lieutenants, as well as many lesser officeholders and politicians.

When ordered by Mayor William Dever to explain why he had attended the dinner, Hughes told him that he was under the impression that the dinner was being held in honor of Jerry O'Connor. "But when I arrived," he said, "and recognized a number of notorious characters I had thrown into the detective bureau basement a half-dozen times, I knew I had been framed, and withdrew almost at once."

O'Banion accepted the platinum watch with pleasure, but whoever had purchased the watch had wasted his money on it. Using favors, violence, bribery, kidnapping and bloodshed, O'Banion delivered the Forty-second and Forty-third Wards to the Republican ticket, headed by U.S. senator Charles S. Deneen and Robert E. Crowe, the latter running for reelection as state's attorney. Crowe defeated his Democratic opponent, Michael I. Igoe, nearly two to one.

O'Banion made his fortune after Prohibition came to the land in 1920. By that time, he was already the leader of a successful criminal gang, and his income from the liquor traffic served to make him a very rich man. It was estimated by the police after his death that he had banked over $1 million from alcohol alone. He supplemented his booze earnings with the proceeds from burglaries, payroll robberies and hijackings. At least two of his exploits were noteworthy, even for Chicago. He led his crew of gunmen into the West Side railroad yards and stole $100,000 worth of Canadian whiskey from a freight car, and in 1924, he pulled off the famous robbery of the Sibley warehouse, carrying out 1,750 barrels of whiskey and leaving identical barrels of water in their place. He was indicted for this, along with ten of his men, four city detectives and officials from the Sibley Warehouse Co. No one was ever convicted.

In 1922, O'Banion bought a half interest in William Schofield's flower shop on North State Street in downtown Chicago. It was located directly across the street from Holy Name Cathedral, where O'Banion once sang in the choir. As gangland's official florist, he sold thousands of dollars' worth of flowers to the friends and foes of slain gunmen, for it was considered good underworld etiquette to send expensive floral tributes to the funeral of your victim. Even without his gangland business, ownership of the flower shop would have made O'Banion wealthy. He had considerable business acumen and a consuming love for flowers. He had a knack for making beautiful arrangements, and his bouquets were considered works of art.

For three years, O'Banion stayed in the good graces of Johnny Torrio, taking part in a truce that left him with Chicago's North Side. But after Torrio and Capone took over Cicero, he began to express some dissatisfaction with the arrangement. Several of his men had supported Capone during the election-day rioting in this West Side city, and O'Banion had gotten nothing out of it but a word of thanks. To placate him, Torrio turned over a strip of Cicero territory that was worth about $20,000 a month. O'Banion soon quintupled this business by persuading about fifty saloonkeepers on the South and West Sides to move into Cicero, where they competed with saloons that were supplied by Torrio and Capone. Torrio demanded a share of this new revenue, and in return, he offered O'Banion an interest in the syndicate's earnings from brothels. O'Banion refused because he was morally offended by dealings in prostitution. During the tenure of the O'Banion operation (and later the Weiss and Moran gangs), not one professional brothel operated in the gang's territory on the North Side of Chicago.

O'Banion also had a grievance against Torrio's allies, the Genna brothers—Sam, Jim, Pete, Angelo, Tony and Mike—who were known as the "Terrible Gennas." O'Banion claimed that the Gennas were moving in on his territory and flooding it with bad whiskey, which they were selling for three dollars per barrel. O'Banion was used to getting six to nine dollars for his barrels, but they were of much better quality. He demanded that Torrio move the Gennas back to the West Side, and when Torrio told him that he couldn't force the brothers to move, O'Banion angrily threatened to do it himself. This was a task that no one but the fiery O'Banion would have dared, for the Gennas and their gunmen were among the most feared in the city.

Five of the six Gennas were typical Sicilian killers—overbearing, savage, treacherous and dangerous and at the same time, devoutly religious. They went regularly to church and carried rosaries and crucifixes in their pockets, right next to their guns. The exception was Tony, known as "Tony the Gentleman," who studied architecture and built model tenements for the poor. He was a patron of the opera and lived elegantly in a downtown hotel. He never killed but attended all family councils, at which murders were planned, and had a voice in all decisions. The Gennas' main gunmen were as dangerous as Tony was civilized. They included Sam "Smoots" Amatuna, an accomplished musician and murderer; Giuseppe Nerone; and the ferocious killers John Scalisi and Albert Anselmi, who were known for teaching Chicago gangsters to run their bullets with garlic to increase the chances of gangrene.

The Gennas put hundreds of poverty-stricken Sicilians and Italians to work cooking corn sugar alcohol in the West Side tenements around Taylor Street. The cookeries and stills produced thousands of gallons of raw alcohol, which was cut, flavored, colored and sold as brandy and whiskey. They made over $350,000 a month, and the lucrative business was protected by Torrio, who received a monthly sum. Federal agents who investigated the Gennas obtained

The "Terrible Gennas" at dinner. *Left to right*: San, Angelo, Peter, Tony and Jim.

a confession from their office manager, who said that five police captains were on the Genna payroll. He also said that four hundred uniformed policemen, mostly from the nearby Maxwell Street station, along with plainclothes officers from headquarters and the state's attorney's office, called at the Genna warehouse each month to collect their own bribes. In addition, the police received their alcohol at discounted prices.

To show his contempt for the Gennas, and for Torrio's leadership, O'Banion hijacked a Genna truck that was loaded with more than $30,000 in whiskey. The Gennas immediately made plans to retaliate but were restrained by Torrio and Mike Merlo, president of the Unione Siciliana and one of the most powerful men in Chicago. Merlo was an important figure, and among his countrymen, his word was law.

He was closely associated with Torrio, Capone and other Sicilian and Italian gangsters but took no part in gang wars and was strongly opposed to murder. Both he and Torrio believed that peace could be made with O'Banion without violence.

Torrio constantly tried to negotiate with O'Banion, but the North Side mobster refused to be swayed. Dozens of meetings were held between Torrio, Capone and O'Banion, and each ended with the same result. O'Banion always promised to recognize the territory of the Gennas and then turned around and hijacked another truck. The Gennas wanted to hit O'Banion, and so did Capone, but Torrio asked them to wait. Torrio knew that if he killed O'Banion, it would mean all-out war in Chicago.

Torrio's hesitation backfired on him in May 1924, when O'Banion came to him and told him that he wanted to sell Torrio his largest

Johnny Torrio, whom O'Banion tricked into buying a brewery that was about to be raided by the police. This stunt, along with some slurs that he made about his Italian competition, likely led to O'Banion's death. *Courtesy of the* Chicago's American.

gambling den and his favorite brewery, Sieben's. He had a good excuse for doing so, claiming that he planned to retire from bootlegging and work in his flower shop.

Torrio agreed to buy up O'Banion's concerns and reportedly paid him a half million dollars in cash two days later. The gang leaders agreed to meet at the Sieben's Brewery on May 19. As it turned out, the brewery was raided that night under the command of Chief of Police Morgan Collins and Captain Matthew Zimmer. Thirteen trucks stacked high with beer barrels were confiscated, and twenty-eight gangsters were arrested, including O'Banion, Hymie Weiss and Torrio. Instead of taking the prisoners to the police station, Chief Collins turned them over to federal authorities. This was Torrio's second arrest for violating Prohibition. He had been arrested once and fined in June 1923, but a second arrest could mean jail time—a fact of which O'Banion had been very much aware. Torrio also realized that O'Banion had no intention of retiring. He had conned Torrio into buying a brewery that he knew the police were about to shut down.

Torrio provided bail money for himself and his gunmen but declined to furnish bonds for O'Banion and Weiss, neither of whom had the necessary money on hand. Torrio suspected treachery and, later, obtained proof that O'Banion had double-crossed him. Through political connections, O'Banion had learned of the raid and had taken advantage of the knowledge to unload his share of the brewery on Torrio and Capone. O'Banion also knew that the prosecution would be handled by the U.S. District Court and that Torrio's influence did not extend to the federal level. He knew he would be fined, but he also knew that Torrio would be in much deeper trouble.

Among Torrio's dominant traits, which accounted for his success as a criminal, was the ability to control his temper. Undoubtedly, he hated O'Banion, but he went about his business as though nothing had happened, since he was aware of the fact that killing O'Banion would result in a bloody war, which would be bad for business.

But O'Banion soon made things worse. He was amused by the "prank" that he had pulled on Torrio, but a shrewd Hymie Weiss urged him to make peace with Torrio and the Gennas. O'Banion laughed at the idea, calling them "gutter rats" and saying with contempt, "To hell with them Sicilians!" This phrase, repeated by O'Banion gunmen as a bit of clever repartee, signed O'Banion's death warrant, for to Sicilians and Italians alike, it was a deadly insult.

Several times during the summer of 1924, the murder of O'Banion was planned by Torrio, Capone and the Gennas, but each time they were stopped by Mike Merlo, who still hoped for a peaceful settlement. But Merlo died from cancer on November 8, 1924—and two days later, Dion O'Banion lay dead among his flowers.

Merlo's funeral was an imposing event. More than $100,000 worth of flowers were sent to his home by friends, and they filled not only the house but the lawn outside as well. The most impressive of these pieces was a statue of the dead man, made entirely of flowers, which stood twelve feet high. Many of the flowers came from O'Banion's shop, including a $10,000 order from Torrio and an $8,000 order from Capone. On November 9, James Genna and Carmen Vacco entered O'Banion's flower shop and ordered a wreath for Merlo's funeral. They gave O'Banion $750 to pay for the arrangement. They told him that they would send some boys to pick it up the next day. Then they left the shop.

On the morning of November 10, the telephone rang, and an unknown caller wanted to know if O'Banion had the wreath ready. He stated that it could be picked up at noon, and at five minutes past the hour, a blue Jewett touring car pulled up in front of the shop.

One of the shop's employees, a black man named William Crutchfield, was sweeping up flower petals in the back room and looked up to see three men get out of the car and walk into the shop. Another man remained at the wheel of the car outside.

O'Banion, dressed in a long white smock and holding a pair of florist's shears in his left hand, came out from behind the counter and extended his hand in greeting. He said, "Hello, boys, you from Mike Merlo's?"

The three men walked abreast and approached O'Banion with smiles on their faces. The man in the center was tall and clean-shaven and wore an expensive overcoat and fedora. It was determined years later that this man was Frankie Yale. The other two, believed to be John Scalise and Albert Anselmi, were shorter and stockier, with dark complexions.

Crutchfield heard the man thought to be Frankie Yale reply, "Yes, for Merlo's flowers." He then stepped closer to O'Banion. Yale grabbed O'Banion's hand in greeting and pulled the other man toward him.

Schofield's Flower Shop in downtown Chicago, of which O'Banion owned a portion.
He was shot to death there in November 1924, setting off an all-out gang war in the city.
Courtesy of the Chicago Daily News.

The two men at his sides moved around O'Banion and drew pistols. Then, at close range, Yale rammed his own pistol into O'Banion's stomach and, holding his arm in a vice-like grip, opened fire. The other two men also fired their weapons, and the bullets ripped into O'Banion. Two slugs struck him in the right breast, two hit him in the throat and one passed through each side of his face. The shots were fired at such close range that powder burns were found at the opening of each wound. From that point on, this method of murder became known as the "Chicago Handshake."

O'Banion fell, dead on his feet, into a display of geraniums. The gang leader had carried three pistols on his person at all times, but they were unfired, not even drawn. The three men fled from the store and climbed into the car outside, which drove slowly away from the scene.

The Genna brothers, Capone and Torrio were all arrested on suspicion of homicide but were soon released after supplying airtight alibis. Frankie Yale was arrested at the La Salle train station, departing for points unknown, but he was also released. The investigation, headed by ace Detective Captain William "Shoes" Shoemaker, went nowhere.

At an elaborate funeral service, O'Banion's friends filed past his body. The tough gangsters wept as they walked into Sbarbaro's Funeral Home. O'Banion was placed inside a $10,000 bronze casket that had been fitted with bronze and silver double walls. A heavy plate-glass window had been fitted over O'Banion's patched-up face, and his men could peer down and see his head where it reclined on a white satin pillow.

O'Banion's funeral was the most lavish in Chicago gangland history. The hearse was led to Mount Carmel Cemetery by twenty-six trucks filled with flowers worth more than $50,000. The scene at the cemetery was even more bizarre. On one side of the grave, lowering the body to rest, were O'Banion's friends, Hymie Weiss, George Moran and Vincent Drucci; on the other were Al Capone, Johnny Torrio and Angelo Genna. The men glared at one another, but no words, or violence, were exchanged.

Cardinal Mundelein had refused to allow funeral services to be held over the dead gangster, but at the grave, a priest who had known O'Banion since childhood recited a litany, a Hail Mary and the Lord's Prayer. The gangster was originally buried in unconsecrated ground but was moved five months after his death to his final resting place. The circumstance of the move prompted Captain John Stege, an honest cop who battled gangsters for years, to say, "O'Banion was a thief and a murderer, but look at him now, buried eighty feet from a bishop."

Some might say that O'Banion did not rest in peace. His murder began the most violent and bloodiest time in Chicago's history, leading to hundreds of deaths and culminating in the horrific St. Valentine's Day Massacre in February 1929.

DEATH ON THE CATHEDRAL STEPS

THE LAST STAND OF EARL "HYMIE" WEISS

For two years after the death of North Side gang leader Dion O'Banion, Vincent "Schemer" Drucci and Earl "Hymie" Weiss played a dangerous game with Al Capone and his well-armed gang of South Side gunmen. There was little chance for Dion O'Banion's successors to do more than maintain the territorial boundaries that already existed, but Drucci and Weiss were motivated by revenge and wanted to strike back at those who had slain O'Banion.

Weiss struck hard at the South Side Outfit first, wounding Johnny Torrio outside of his home. Torrio survived the attack, and after serving jail time for earlier liquor charges, he fled Chicago, leaving his criminal empire to Al Capone. Capone was now the top man in Chicago, but he had a bloody gang war on his hands.

Hymie Weiss offered to stem further violence if Capone handed John Scalise and Albert Anselmi over to him. It was a poorly kept secret that they had been in the flower shop when O'Banion was murdered. Capone refused and made plans to knock off Hymie Weiss instead. He was too slow, though. Weiss and George Moran had already planned their next move.

On May 26, 1925, they murdered Angelo Genna, one of Capone's supporters. A month later, Mike Genna was killed by the police as he, John Scalise and Albert Anselmi were about to ambush George Moran. Scalise and Anselmi killed two police officers before escaping. Tony Genna was murdered soon after by the Gennas' own

Earl "Hymie" Weiss took over Dion O'Banion's operations after his boss was murdered. Weiss himself was gunned down outside of Holy Name Cathedral on October 11, 1926—directly across the street from where O'Banion was killed. *Courtesy of the* Chicago Daily News.

Vincent "the Schemer" Drucci helped Hymie Weiss run the North Side mob and was almost killed alongside his friend during the so-called Battle of Michigan Avenue, which was waged outside of the Standard Oil Building. Drucci was later killed by a police officer during the mayoral elections in April 1927. *Courtesy of* Chicago's American.

gunman, Giuseppe Nerone, who may have been paid by Capone to assassinate him in an effort to stem the bloodshed. The surviving Gennas soon left for Italy.

Capone retaliated next. He marked Drucci and Weiss for death and assigned gunman Louis Barko to carry out the murders on August 10, 1926. The event became known as the "Battle of Michigan Avenue."

Drucci maintained a residence at the Congress Hotel, four blocks north of the Standard Oil Building at Ninth Street and Michigan Avenue. On the morning of August 10, following a late breakfast, Weiss and Drucci met at the Congress and walked toward the Standard Oil Building, where they were to meet with Morris Eller, a Sanitary District trustee. Eller was the mobbed-up boss of the Twentieth Ward and a cheap racketeer who offered a presentable face as a politician. Drucci was carrying $13,200 in cash in his pockets, which was allegedly a down payment on a piece of real estate but was more likely bribe money for the North Side gang's Twentieth Ward sponsors.

As Drucci and Weiss were about to pass through the Neo–Italian Renaissance doors of the building, Louis Barko and three other men jumped out of a car on the east side of Michigan Avenue and opened fire on them. Windows shattered, and bullets chipped at stone walls as Drucci scrambled for cover behind parked cars. Weiss managed to get into the lobby of the building, shaken but unhurt.

Drucci pulled out his own gun and returned fire before commandeering an automobile that belonged to C.C. Bassett, a startled motorist who had been trapped in the crossfire. Drucci's escape was interrupted by the arrival of the police, who dragged him off the car's running board. The affair turned out to be a bloodless one, and it was over in less than two minutes.

When questioned by the police at the South Clark Street station, Drucci denied knowing Barko and dismissed the whole thing as an attempted robbery. Hymie Weiss's mother, Mary, posted the necessary bond and freed her son's friend from behind bars.

Drucci was lucky that day, but his luck didn't hold for long. In April 1927, he was shot to death by Detective Sergeant Daniel F. Healy on the eve of the city's mayoral election. Police radio cars had issued orders to arrest all gangsters on sight, and while making the rounds on the North Side, Healy and his squad spotted Drucci, who was carrying a gun. Feeling harassed, Drucci chided Healy and the other officers and allegedly threatened them. The altercation turned violent, and Drucci attacked the detective, who had a gun in the gangster's rib cage. Healy shot him four times, and Drucci was dead before he hit the sidewalk. Al Capone couldn't be blamed for this one.

After the shootout at the Standard Oil Building, the opposing gangs agreed to a peace conference. Capone again denied Weiss's request to mete out punishment to O'Banion's killers, so Weiss and George Moran led a hasty assault on Capone's club, the Four Deuces, at 2222 South Wabash. Capone somehow escaped unhurt, but his driver, Tony Ross, died behind the wheel.

A week later, on September 20, 1926, Weiss pulled another crazy stunt, this time sealing his fate. He sent a caravan of motor cars, each carrying a trio of machine gunners, to Capone's Cicero headquarters, the Hawthorne Inn. Seated at a table in the crowded coffee shop, Capone was thrown to the floor by his bodyguard as the first volley of shots was fired into the storefront. The hotel was riddled with bullets, but Capone escaped death again.

That violent incident was Weiss's one moment of glory and revenge for O'Banion's murder. And while he continued to live a fearless life (to the point of stupidity) and to goad Capone at every opportunity, his days were numbered.

On October 11, Weiss was attending the murder trial of "Polack Joe" Saltis and his driver, Frank "Lefty" Koncil, and decided to take a break and return to his office above O'Banion's old flower shop. As Weiss and gunman Patrick Murray drove toward the office, they had no idea that four machine gunners were waiting for them. These men, believed to be John Scalise, Albert Anselmi, Frank Diamond and Frank Nitti, were hiding on the third floor of a nearby building. Weiss was a marked man as soon as he left his car on Superior Street, just south of Holy Name Cathedral. He approached the flower shop with Murray by his side, and at the deafening sound of Tommy guns, the pedestrians on the street scattered.

Murray died instantly, but Weiss took ten bullets and survived long enough to be pronounced dead at Henrotin Hospital without regaining consciousness. The bullets that killed Weiss tore away portions of the inscription on the church's cornerstone and left bullet holes as a graphic reminder of the event. The church tried to obliterate them years later, but the chips and marks remain. They can still be seen on the corner of the cathedral today.

Meanwhile, the assassins fled their third-floor lair, exited the rear of the building and disappeared into the crowds along Dearborn Street. A discarded machine gun was found in an alley off Dearborn, but it couldn't be traced back to the killers.

One has to wonder how hard the police looked for them. Chief Morgan Collins issued a gruff statement: "I don't want to encourage the business, but if somebody has to be killed, it's a good thing the gangsters are murdering themselves off. It saves trouble for the police."

THE MAN THEY NEVER HANGED

One of the oddest tales in the annals of Chicago crime is the story of "Terrible" Tommy O'Connor, a lowlife, small-time crook who never would have made a mark in history except for the fact that the old Chicago gallows were kept waiting for him for more than fifty years after he was sentenced to hang. The rotting timbers remained in storage in the Cook County jail—just in case O'Connor was ever captured. By the time they were finally removed from the basement of the jail in 1977, the state had long since switched to the electric chair for executions. But O'Connor had escaped from prison and disappeared in 1921. He had been sentenced to hang within the precincts of the old jail, and if he were ever captured, the sentence would have had to be carried out.

Tommy O'Connor became a mythical figure in Chicago history, and a portrait of him still hangs in the atrium of the old Criminal Courts building. But how did a petty thug, universally disliked by police officers and fellow criminals, become one of the most unusual characters in Windy City crime?

O'Connor was born in Ireland but moved to Chicago with his family when he was only two years old. He grew up in the West Side Maxwell Street neighborhood, a notoriously bad area that was so riddled with crime that reporters dubbed it "Bloody Maxwell." His immigrant father worked hard, putting in enough long hours to be able to move his family to a small house near Thirteenth Street and

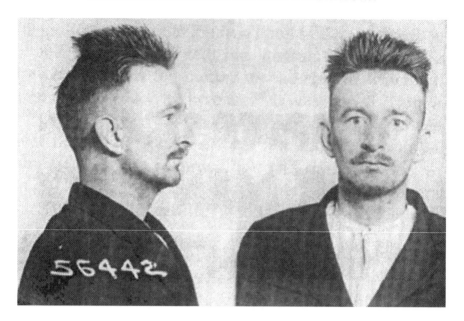

The mug shot of "Terrible" Tommy O'Connor. *Courtesy of Adam Selzer.*

Paulina Avenue. But even in these better surroundings, Tommy still managed to fall in with a bad crowd. He and his best friend, Jimmy Cherin, began hanging out in local saloons, where they became fascinated with stories told about automobile thieves. Motor cars were still a novelty in those days, and to an impressionable boy like Tommy, automobile theft seemed like a daring and glamorous crime.

Tommy and Jimmy were especially enthralled by the stories of Trilby Thompson, an early car thief from whose methods O'Connor learned a lot. Eventually, the police offered a $5,000 reward for Thompson, and the criminal answered the inquiry himself. Thompson sent a note to the police, giving him his location and taunting them to "come and take me. I am dying, but I'd like to kill a few policemen first."

O'Connor was excited by a potential life of crime and began to get involved in minor holdups and robberies. He earned a nasty reputation as a man quick with a gun. During one holdup, O'Connor was told by the leader of the gang that there would be no shooting. O'Connor shot the robbery victim anyway and told the leader that he did it because he felt like it, and he would shoot the boss too if he didn't like it. When Chicago Police Sergeant Herman Otten killed a bandit friend of O'Connor's named Jimmy Higgins, O'Connor sent a letter to Otten promising to kill him.

O'Connor continued his sordid career for about two years and then was arrested for the first time. He was indicted for the murder of a robbery victim, and even though one of the members of his own gang testified against him, the prosecution was unable to make to make the charges stick. O'Connor was set free.

After being released, O'Connor was bitter toward the man who testified against him, another lowlife named Emerson. After stewing about it for several days, O'Connor went to see his old friend Jimmy Cherin. The two had spent their youths committing crimes and dreaming of becoming important criminals, and now O'Connor asked Cherin to help him kill Emerson. Jimmy refused. He had since gone straight and was married with a newborn child. No one knows what words were exchanged between the two men, but it has been surmised that Cherin not only turned O'Connor down but also may have threatened to tell what he knew to the police.

Cherin's refusal sealed his fate. O'Connor shot his longtime friend five times, killing him in his own home. He was indicted for murder but, once again, was never brought to trial. The murder also claimed two more victims. A short time later, Jimmy's wife, insane with grief, killed herself and her baby.

By March 1920, O'Connor had killed at least five men. Late one night, a squad of police detectives raided the home of O'Connor's brother-in-law, where O'Connor was lying low after a string of robberies. The police had a warrant and were looking for him due to bond forfeiture related to the death of Jimmy Cherin.

When the police burst into the home, O'Connor grabbed his gun and began firing wildly. Five shots rang out, and a bullet struck Chicago detective Sergeant Patrick "Paddy" O'Neill in the chest. O'Neill died half an hour later. In the mêlée, O'Connor escaped, managing to slip past uniformed policemen who were looking for him less than fifty feet away. Tommy O'Connor was "on the lam."

For the next four months, the police hunted for O'Connor all over the United States in what was said to be the most extensive manhunt in the history of the Chicago force. They followed numerous false leads until finally tracking him down aboard a train to Omaha. He was drunk and held up the porter who had sold him the beer. The train was stopped in St. Paul, Minnesota, and O'Connor escaped. As he jumped down onto the tracks, he pulled out a gun and tried to board the switch engine of another train, only to be kept off that train by a fireman who swung an axe at him. He ran alongside the tracks on foot for a while before being captured by a switch foreman on the Chicago–Great Western passenger line. He was only arrested for being drunk and disorderly but made the mistake of telling the St. Paul police who he was.

Within days, he was back in Chicago, where he claimed his innocence in the shooting of the police officer. "It wasn't my revolver that killed [O'Neill]," he said. "[He] was shot by his own pals. A mistake, of course, but they shot him. And after that mistake they ran away and put the blame on me. What chance had I with every policeman in the city out to get me dead or alive?"

Not surprisingly, no one believed his story. O'Connor was tried, convicted, sentenced to hang and sent to jail to await his execution. But on December 11, 1921, a few days before he was to be hanged, he escaped.

While talking with a prison guard about getting a pass to go to the hospital, O'Connor and three others overpowered guard David Straus with a pistol that had been smuggled in by an accommodating prison cook. They beat Straus, tied him up and took his key. As they made their way through the jail, they were surprised by another guard but managed to subdue him as well. The escapees made their way to the roof, where they jumped nine feet down into an alley. The jump was too much for one of the prisoners; he broke both of his ankles when he landed on the ground and made it no farther.

The other three men ran north up the alley to Illinois Street, where they jumped onto the running boards of an automobile and ordered the driver to keep driving. A guard from the jail chased after them, almost snagging O'Connor's shirt with an outstretched hand. But O'Connor pistol-whipped him, knocking him away, and the car sped away. This was the last the law ever saw of "Terrible" Tommy O'Connor.

Huge rewards for O'Connor's capture were offered. At one point, offers were made to a newspaper from underworld characters to secure an interview with Tommy in exchange for a large sum of money and immunity. The newspaper took the deal but hastily backed out of it. It worried that any reporter who gained information on Tommy O'Connor wasn't likely to live long.

O'Connor was never found. Rumors circulated for years that he was somewhere on the South Side, under the protection of friends. Others say that he fled the country and went to Ireland. Many reports from the 1930s stated that he became a part of the Touhy gang, a group of Chicago toughs and kidnappers led by Roger Touhy that included the infamous "Pretty Boy" Floyd for a time. The gang started kidnapping prominent citizens, mostly labor big shots, and holding them for ransom. Eventually, several labor leaders had to be guarded by federal authorities.

For decades, rumors about O'Connor's whereabouts came to the attention of the police every couple of months. Practically every year, the newspapers would run stories about the legendary escape. All the while, the gallows were kept in the basement of the prison, just in case. When the prison was torn down and the prisoners moved to a facility on Twenty-sixth Street and California Avenue, the gallows went with them.

As more years passed, the chance that O'Connor would be captured began to fade. Some still believed that one day he would be found, and when he was, the gallows would be brought back to the vicinity of the old jail, which was a parking lot by then, and set up with canvas walls around them. There, Tommy would swing at last.

Fewer and fewer people believed that would happen. Even if O'Connor were caught, there would surely be appeals. After all, many years had passed since his escape. Judge Kickham Scanlan, who had sentenced him, was long dead. Harry Stanton, the jail plumber who had built the scaffolds for sixty-five men, had retired in 1927 after twenty-nine years. And in 1964, the warden said that the gallows had rotted and would be impossible to use for a hanging. If O'Connor were alive at all, he had outlived the gallows themselves.

But the gallows, decayed or not, remained in storage until 1977, when workers clearing out the basement of the court building came upon the beams and bolts, piled high in a corner. They asked Chief Criminal Court Judge Richard J. Fitzgerald if they could dispose of them once and for all. After all, Tommy was surely dead by then. The judge said he would sign a court order to have them destroyed. "Heck," he said, "under present laws we couldn't execute the guy even if he surrendered tomorrow." But he suggested setting the gallows up one last time just to see what they looked like.

Workers managed to assemble the gallows, and they added a fresh rope to them, along with a sign that read, "Tired of waiting, Tommy." After that, the gallows were dismantled for the final time.

Tommy O'Connor, if he managed to survive, had officially escaped the noose.

THE END OF JAKE LINGLE

The murder of Jake Lingle, a sixty-five-dollar-a-week crime reporter for the *Chicago Tribune*, was the biggest crime sensation of 1930. The public, which had never heard of him, assumed that he had been shot to death because he knew too much about the gangsters who seemed to have a firm grip on the city and was about to divulge their dirty laundry in the press.

A week or two after his murder, it was learned that he was not only friends with the gangsters he was allegedly going to expose but he was also profiting off of them. Lingle lived like a king in a suite at the Stevens Hotel and kept a second home on Lake Michigan. He kept a secret bank account at the Lake Shore Trust and Savings totaling $63,900—which was not bad for a reporter making $65 a week. When details of his bank account and lavish lifestyle were announced, it caused great embarrassment and bad publicity for the *Tribune*, which billed itself as "the world's greatest newspaper." The *Tribune* had turned Lingle into a martyr of the free press but soon regretted its hasty decision to do so.

The case, despite the huge reward that was offered, began to take on a suspicious odor and was never really solved to the satisfaction of many involved. Questions remain unanswered as to what sort of deal was offered to the man who took responsibility for the murder and what damage could have been done to certain politicians with

Jake Lingle, the notorious *Chicago Tribune* reporter who was murdered in 1930. *Courtesy of* Chicago's American.

Chicago killer Frank McErlane was one of the victims of the violence that rocked Chicago in the early months of 1930. He was nearly killed in his hospital room, but a convenient gun under his pillow helped him to hold off his would-be killers. *Courtesy of* Chicago's American.

ties to the underworld if certain aspects of Lingle's activities had come to light.

The case would have one positive outcome, however: it finally turned public opinion against Al Capone, and the other Chicago gangs, once and for all.

The final months of 1929 were relatively quiet in Chicago. The St. Valentine's Day Massacre, which took place earlier in the year, had produced an eerie calm in the city. Capone was now firmly in control, and few dared to challenge him. By the later months of 1929, there had been only fifty-three gangland murders in Chicago, a number that, while still nothing to be bragged about by city leaders, was far below that of the previous year. There was, during that summer, even time for relaxing and social life, allowing the gangsters to come out of hiding and mix with their friends and families. When a relative of Capone partner Jake Guzik was married, there was a great gathering at the church that included Bathhouse John Coughlin, alderman of the First Ward; William V. Pacelli, alderman of the Twentieth Ward; Captain of Police Hugh McCarthy; and Ralph Capone. Al himself could not be present since he was detained in Philadelphia at the time, the result of a put-up job by the national syndicate to keep him out of the spotlight for a while.

Only a couple of bloody incidents marred the early months of 1930. In January, a gun battle occurred in which Frank McErlane received partial payback for the murders of at least nine victims of gangland slayings for which he was reportedly responsible. Coroners had often listed him as a cause of death. He was also indicted for the double killing of George Bucher and George Meeghan, but the charges were dismissed. McErlane had been getting restless. He had fought over shares with his partner, Joe Saltis, and had transferred his allegiance to the South Side O'Donnells.

On the night of January 28, McErlane was attacked, and his right leg was fractured by a bullet. While recovering at the German Deaconess Hospital, he had two unexpected visitors, who walked into his room and opened fire. McErlane, imprisoned by splints, did the best he could. He reached under his pillow and pulled out a .38-caliber revolver, which he fired five times. The intruders ran, leaving McErlane alive. Two full chambers had been fired at him, but McErlane was only hit three times and none of the wounds was fatal.

He was interviewed by the police but, of course, did not name his attackers. He did, however, hint angrily that this would not be the end of the matter. One of the gunmen had been John "Dingbat" O'Berta (an Italian gangster who had inserted an Irish apostrophe into his name), a ferocious little man who was Saltis's chief gunman. On March 5, O'Berta and his driver, Sam Malaga, were taken for a ride in Dingbat's own Lincoln sedan. O'Berta had been shotgunned to death. His funeral was a two-day wake attended by fifteen thousand admirers from the Back-of-the-Yards district on the South Side, where O'Berta had earned a name for himself as an influential young politician.

Dingbat's widow had previously been the wife of Big Tim Murphy, the racketeer controller of the Street Sweeper's Union who had been machine-gunned in front of his Rogers Park home in June 1928. She and O'Berta had met at Murphy's funeral. She had her second husband buried next to her first in Holy Sepulchre Cemetery; each held a rosary in his gun hand. She told reporters, "They were both good men."

In the last week of May 1930, the guns roared again, kicking off what some wags would dub "Slaughter Week." On Saturday, Peter Gnolfo, who had once worked for the defunct Genna operation and had enlisted with the Aiellos, was shotgunned to death in a spiteful murder that was carried out by the Druggan-Lake gang and attributed to orders from Capone. Within hours, the Aiellos struck back, and three died in the reprisal. A party of five was sitting on the terrace of a small resort hotel on Piskatee Lake during the early hours of Sunday morning. They were Joseph Bertsche, who, since being released from the Atlanta Penitentiary, had been working for the Druggan-Lake mob; Micheal Quirk, a labor racketeer and beer runner; George Druggan, Terry Druggan's brother; Sam Peller, an election strong-arm man from the Twentieth Ward; and Mrs. Vivian McGinnis, the wife of a Chicago lawyer. A full drum of machine-gun bullets shattered the glass and slaughtered the group at the table. Peller, Quirk and Bertshe died on the spot. Druggan and Mrs. McGinnis were both injured. The assailants vanished into the darkness.

No arrest was made, and newspapers explained the attack as a quarrel that had developed because some of the Druggan-Lake boys were muscling in on the Fox Lake area, which was then supplied by Aiello and Moran breweries.

The reprisals continued, and on Tuesday, Thomas Somnerio, an Aiello man, was found dead in an alley at the rear of 831 West Harrison Street in Chicago. He had been garroted, and a deep line around his neck indicated that it had been done slowly in an effort to make him talk. His wrists had been bound with wire.

Four days later, a tugboat passing along the drainage canal at Summit, on the Southwest Side, bumped into the body of Eugene "Red" McLaughlin, a Druggan-Lake gunman who had been named four times as a murderer and twice as a diamond thief yet had never seen the inside of a prison. He had been shot twice in the head and dumped in the river. His wrists had been tied behind his back with telephone wire, and seventy-five pounds of iron had been stuffed in his pockets. It hadn't been enough to keep him from floating up from the bottom of the canal.

Two weeks later, his body was identified by his brother, Bob McLaughlin, who was president of the Chicago Checker Cab Company. He had taken over the office from Joe Wokral, who had run into a nasty accident while running for reelection (he had been shot in the head). Before Wokral died, he named Red McLaughlin as his attacker, a lead that was ignored by the police. A mournful Bob McLaughlin spoke to reporters after the grim task of identifying his brother's corpse. He said, "A better kid never lived. He was friendly with all the boys, the West Side outfit, the North Siders, and the bunch on the South Side, Capone, too...I don't know, I don't know."

On the day after the tugboat nosed McLaughlin's body out of the water, a car driven by a man named Frank R. Thompson steered erratically into a filling station in the small town of New Milford, about ninety miles northwest of Chicago. The door opened, and Thompson, covered in blood, fell to the ground at the feet of the service station attendant, begging the stunned man to call a doctor. Little was known about Thompson. He was a gun dealer who—ballistics tests suggested—had supplied at least one machine gun used in the St. Valentine's Day Massacre and in the killing of Capone enemy Frankie Yale in New York. He was taken, gravely wounded, to Rockford Hospital, where he was interviewed by Sheriff Harry Baldwin. Thompson's dying words were: "Listen, Harry. I've seen everything, done everything and got everything and you're smart enough to know I won't talk. Go to hell."

For most Chicagoans, such a string of murders and violence was commonplace, but on Monday, June 9, a new and apparently different incident became the talk of the town. This outrage was splashed across the front page of every newspaper in the city. Alfred L. "Jake" Lingle, a crime reporter for the *Chicago Tribune*, was shot to death while walking, smoking a cigar and reading the racing news in the crowded underpass at Randolph and Michigan during the lunch hour.

Lingle's death created a furor. In those days, a newspaper reporter was not well paid, but he had a place in public regard that was generated by glamour, respect and authority. The murder of Lingle immediately assumed the importance of that of a public official—and was better publicized by every newspaper in town.

Lingle's duties on the police beat for the *Tribune* earned him sixty-five dollars a week, which was not a princely sum. He had never had a byline in the paper, and his name was unknown to most readers. To the public, he became much more famous in death than he ever was in life. And soon, he became notorious as he was revealed to have had a much larger income than what he could have earned at the paper. He owned a chauffeur-driven Lincoln limousine. He had just bought a $16,000 house at Long Beach on Lake Michigan, where his wife and two children were planning to spend the summer months. He had recently taken a suite at the Stevens, one of Chicago's most stylish hotels. He was also an avid gambler at the horse and greyhound tracks, a vice that was widely known to his newspaper colleagues. They believed that his lavish lifestyle was based on his winnings.

On the day of his death, he was on his way to the races. He had left his wife packing for her departure to the lake house, and he planned to spend the afternoon at Washington Park in Homewood. Later that night, he planned to go to the Sheridan Wave Tournament Club, a society gambling parlor on Waveland Avenue, where champagne, whiskey and food were distributed with the management's compliments during play. It was due to reopen that evening, and Lingle wanted to be there.

In retrospect, it seems that Lingle knew that he was in trouble. Attorney Louis B. Piquett later volunteered to the police that twenty-four hours before Lingle's death, he had met with the reporter in the Loop. They stood on Randolph Street talking about the discovery of

Red McLaughlin's body in the canal. Lingle was giving Piquett his theory of the crime when a blue sedan with two men inside pulled alongside them and stopped at the curb. Lingle stopped talking in midsentence and looked up at the men in a startled way. The two men simply stared at him. Lingle never finished what he was saying to Piquett. He simply told the attorney goodbye and walked into a nearby store. Also, on the day of his murder, after lunching at the Sherman Hotel, he met Sergeant Thomas Alcock of the Detective Bureau and told him that he was being tailed.

Apparently, he was. After buying cigars at the Sherman Hotel kiosk, he walked the four blocks to Michigan Avenue to catch the 1:30 p.m. train to the Washington Park racetrack. He descended the pedestrian subway to enter the Illinois Central suburban electric railroad in Grant Park. At that time of day, the subway was very busy, filled with a steady stream of shoppers and office workers.

Oddly, even though he knew he was being followed, Lingle acted unconcerned. According to witnesses, he arrived at the entrance to the subway walking between two men. One had blond hair and wore a straw boater hat and a gray suit. The other was dark haired and wore a blue suit. At the entrance, Lingle paused and bought a racing edition of the evening newspaper. As he did so, a man in a roadster on the south side of Randolph Street blew his horn to attract Lingle's attention. There were two men in the automobile, and one of them called out, "Play Hy Schneider in the third!" According to a Yellow Cab superintendent who heard the exchange, Lingle grinned, waved at the man and called back, "I've got him!"

Lingle walked on into the subway. He was seen by Dr. Joseph Springer, a former coroner's physician and a longtime acquaintance. Springer later reported, "Lingle didn't see me. He was reading the race information. He was holding it before him with both hands and smoking a cigar."

Lingle had almost reached the end of the subway. He stopped across from the newsstand, about twenty-five feet short of the east exit, and the dark-haired man who had been walking next to him steered away as if to buy a paper. As he did, the blond man stepped behind Lingle, pulled out a snub-nosed .38 colt and fired a single shot into the back of Lingle's head. The single bullet drove upward into his brain and exited his forehead. Lingle pitched forward, cigar still clenched in his teeth and newspaper still in his hands.

The Lingle murder site in the underpass. The reporter's straw boater lies just outside the pool of blood, and his newspaper is crumpled beneath him. *Courtesy of* Chicago's American.

The blond killer tossed away the gun and ran forward into the crowd. Then, for some reason, he doubled back past Lingle's body and ran up the eastern staircase. He jumped a fence, changed his mind again, ran west on Randolph Street, through a passage (where he tossed away a left-handed silk glove, probably used to prevent leaving fingerprints) and, pursued by a policeman, ran onto Wabash Avenue, where he disappeared into the crowd.

Meanwhile, in the subway, Patrick Campbell saw the dark-haired man who had been walking with Lingle and the killer hurrying toward the west exit. Campbell moved to try and catch him, but his movement was blocked by a priest who bumped into him. The man delayed Campbell just long enough for the accomplice to escape, telling Campbell that he was getting out of the subway because someone had been shot. Later, Lieutenant William Cusack of the Detective Bureau commented gruffly, "He was no priest. A priest would never do that. He would have gone to the side of the stricken person."

Slowly, the method of Lingle's murder became clear. He had walked into a trap that had been formed by perhaps as many as a dozen men. But what was never put forward as a theory, and what seems the most likely explanation for the ease in which he walked into the trap, was that during his progress into the subway between the two men, he was eased along by a gun, under orders to keep walking naturally and keep reading the paper.

That evening, Colonel Robert R. McCormick, publisher of the *Chicago Tribune*, summoned his news staff together and addressed them about the death of a reporter he had never met and whose name he had never heard before. He spoke for forty-five minutes and pledged to solve the murder. The next morning, the front page of the paper blared with an eight-inch banner headline that announced the death of Lingle. The story read:

> *Alfred L. Lingle, better known in the world of newspaper work as Jake Lingle, and for the last eighteen years a reporter on the* Tribune, *was shot to death yesterday in the Illinois Central subway at the east side of Michigan Boulevard, at Randolph Street.*
>
> *The* Tribune *offers $25,000 as a reward for information which will lead to the conviction of the slayer or slayers. An additional reward of $5,000 was announced by the* Chicago Evening Post, *making a total of $30,000.*

The next morning, not to be outdone by the *Tribune*, Hearst's *Chicago Herald & Examiner* also offered up a $25,000 reward, bringing the total up to $55,000.

Colonel McCormick, meanwhile, continued to take Lingle's death as an affront to him personally and an attack on the press. He regarded it as being much more serious than the other hundreds of cases of violence that plagued Chicago. He announced that Lingle's murder had been committed in reprisal and as an attempt to intimidate the newspapers into not publishing stories about the dealings of the underworld. But, he declared, this was now a war, and the *Tribune* and Chicago's other newspapers would not rest until Lingle's killers had been brought to justice.

Police Commissioner Russell was forced into making a statement. "I have given orders to the five Deputy Police Commissioners to make this town so quiet that you will be able to hear a consumptive canary cough," he said colorfully, but then he added, as a preliminary explanation for the lack of further action, "Of course, most of the underworld has scuttled off to hiding places. It will be hard to find them, but we will never rest until the criminals are caught and Chicago is free of them forever."

The next day, a newspaper editorial remarked sadly:

> *These gangs have run the town for many months and have strewn the streets with the lacerated bodies of their victims. Commissioner Russell and Deputy Commissioner John P. Stege have had their opportunity to break up there criminal gangs, who have made the streets hideous with bleeding corpses. They have failed.*

Russell replied to the charges, "My conscience is clear. All I ask is that the city will sit tight and see what is going to happen."

All that actually happened was that Russell and Stege, in the words of the newspaper, "staged a mock heroic battle with crime by arresting every dirty-necked ragamuffin on the street corners, but carefully abstained from taking into custody any of the men who matter."

Meanwhile, some of the blanks that had remained in the accounts of Lingle's character and lifestyle began to be filled in. It is fair to say that the management at the *Tribune* was unaware of them; otherwise, it likely would not have turned Lingle into the martyr that it did. Some of the facts that had remained so far unmentioned were that Lingle had been tagged the "unofficial Chief of Police"; he had himself hinted that it was he who fixed the price of beer in Chicago; he was a close friend of Al Capone and had stayed with him at his Florida estate; when he died, he was wearing a diamond-studded belt that had been a gift from Capone; he was improbably, for a newspaper reporter of lowly status, on friendly terms with millionaire businessmen, judges and county and city officials; and he went on golfing holidays and shared stock market tips with the police commissioner, a boyhood chum whom Lingle had helped elevate to his current position in 1928.

By the time a week had passed, certain reservations had started to temper the anger that had been displayed on the front page and in the editorial columns of the *Tribune*. As more details about Lingle's extracurricular activities began to emerge, McCormick and his editorial executives began to backpedal away from the earlier statements and demands. The word-of-mouth buzz about Lingle's background and liaisons was racing around Chicago, supported by muckraking stories in other newspapers, and the *Tribune* began to take a different stance. The paper admitted that Lingle was apparently involved in some unsavory activity but noted that the gangsters who killed him were still out there—and still needed to be brought to justice.

McCormick's investigators, as well as the police, had learned a lot about the background of Jake Lingle, a semiprofessional baseball player from the slums who had wormed his way into the lowest levels of Chicago journalism. His first job after leaving a West Jackson Boulevard elementary school was as an office boy at a surgical supply house. He was playing semiprofessional baseball at the time and met Bill Russell, a police patrolman, with whom he struck up a friendship. Lingle was hired as a *Tribune* copy boy in 1918. He had no aptitude for writing, but it was his long list of contacts (mostly made through Russell) and timely telephone calls to the city desk that made him indispensable to editors and rewrite men. The brash and cocky reporter cultivated acquaintances in the courts, jails and gin mills of the North and South Sides. Relying on the word of informants and friendships, he became one of the city's least known but most clever crime reporters. He also became one of the wealthiest, but whether this was from his dealings in the stock market, his investments in gambling clubs on the North Side or some other source is unknown.

Some believed that Lingle operated as a liaison between the underworld and the city's political machine. Many out of town newspapers were referring to the slain reporter as the "unofficial Chief of Police," implying that he had maintained a close relationship with many city hall insiders, including attorney Samuel A. Ettleson, the corporation counsel for Chicago and an operator in city government.

Al Capone confirmed that Lingle was a close friend and "one of the boys" during an interview in Florida in July 1930. He said that he had not had any sort of disagreement with Lingle that led to his death. Capone also stated, "The Chicago police know who killed him."

The question of who killed Jake Lingle was temporarily forgotten during the exposure of his fascinating financial affairs. In addition to the secret bank account that Lingle kept with the Lake Shore Trust and Savings Bank, he was also known for carrying large sums of cash in his pocket. He had $9,000 on him the day he was killed. Another interesting branch of his activities that came to light were his "loans" from gamblers, politicians and businessmen. He had "borrowed" $2,000 from Jimmy Mondi, a Capone gambling operator in Cicero and the Loop—a loan that had never been paid back. He had borrowed $5,000 from Alderman Berthold A. Cronson, nephew of Samuel Ettleson, who later stated that the loan was a "pure friendship proposition." It had also never been repaid. Additionally, he had borrowed $5,000 from Ettleson himself, who only said that he had never given money to Lingle but often gave him some small remembrance at Christmas. He had taken a loan of $2,500 from Carolos Ames, president of the Civil Service Commission, which Ames stated was a "purely personal affair." He had also borrowed $300 from Police Lieutenant Thomas McFarland, who said that he had given Lingle the money because they had been close friends for many years. It was also alleged that Sam Hare, a roadhouse and gambling parlor operator, had "loaned" Lingle $20,000. Hare denied the accusation.

Investigations revealed that Lingle had been in an investment partnership with his old friend, Police Commissioner Russell. The account, used for stock market speculation, was opened in November 1928 with a $20,000 deposit. On September 20, 1929—preceding the market crash in October—the joint paper profits were $23,696. Later, a loss of $58,850 was shown. Linger showed paper profits at a peak of $85,000, which, after the crash, were converted to a loss of $75,000. Russell's losses were variously reported as $100,000 and $250,000.

As to the source of the money put up by Lingle in the account and deposited into his bank account, investigators noted, "We have thus far been able to come to no conclusion."

But the press and the public had come to conclusions, and they were painfully obvious ones, which again confirmed that they were the residents of a city governed by dishonorable leaders and corrupt officials. The newspapers theorized about why Lingle had been murdered, but the fervor—and righteous anger—had waned. Lingle had "asked for it," so to speak, by becoming involved with gangsters and dirty politicians.

Most theories of his death identified Lingle as a favor seller, and most placed the blame on Capone's opposition, the Moran-Aiello merger. One story that made the rounds in gangland was that Lingle had been given $50,000 to secure protection for a West Side dog track, which he had failed to do and instead kept the money.

Another story implicated him in the reopening of the Sheridan Wave Tournament Club, which had been operated by the Weiss-Moran gang, but which, after the St. Valentine's Day Massacre, had closed. Moran worked for eighteen months to try and find sympathetic officials to help him reopen the club, giving the job to Joe Josephs and Julian "Potatoes" Kaufman. It was said that Kaufman, an old friend of Lingle, had approached him and asked him to use his influence with the police to get the club open again. Allegedly, it was agreed to—but only if Lingle was cut in on the action. He demanded 50 percent of the profits, but Kaufman refused. Lingle then retorted, "If this joint is opened up, you'll see more squad cars in front ready to raid it than you ever saw in your life before." In spite of this, the story said, the club reopened, and it was widely advertised that it would be opening on June 9, the day on which Lingle set out for the races for the final time.

An equally plausible story stated that Lingle got too deeply involved in the struggle for money and power in the gambling syndicate. For years, there had been a bitter war between the General News Bureau, a racing news wire service that existed entirely for the purposes of betting, and the independent news services. As an appointed intermediary, Lingle brought the two opposed factions together in

Leo Brothers, the St. Louis gunman who was convicted of the Jake Lingle murder. Most crime historians feel that he was encouraged to take the fall for the crime to protect underworld figures and politicians in Chicago. *Courtesy of* Chicago's American.

January 1930, and a two-year truce was agreed on. The truce, it was said, may not have extended to Lingle.

Any of these stories could have been true, or they could all have missed the mark. Whatever the reason behind his murder, Lingle likely just got mixed up in the violence and bloodshed of gangland, an arena where even the most experienced can sometimes be torn apart. However, the biggest question remained: who pulled the trigger that ended the reporter's life?

Weeks and then months passed before the police produced a suspect. The serial number on the handgun that the killer had dropped was filed away, but ballistics expert Colonel Calvin Goddard traced the origin of the gun to a sporting goods store owned by Peter Von Frantzius on Diversey Parkway. Records showed that the gun had been sold to Frankie Foster, a member of the North Side Moran gang. Foster fled to Los Angeles after the Lingle shooting but was indicted in Chicago as an accessory before the fact to murder. Foster, whose real name was Frank Citro, was eventually extradited to Chicago and was held in the county jail for four months, but the evidence against him was deemed inconclusive, and the charges were dropped.

A short time later, a new suspect was named. Leo Vincent Brothers, a labor union slugger from St. Louis, was arrested in New York and indicted for the Lingle murder. Brothers had started out as a member of Egan's Rats, a St. Louis gang, and soon graduated into labor racketeering and contract murder. Dodging a 1929 murder indictment, Brothers fled to Chicago, where he found work with Al Capone. Brothers was convicted and sentenced to fourteen years in prison on April 2, 1931.

"I can do that standing on my head!" Brothers quipped after the sentence was handed down. Most observers, then and now, believe that Brothers was handed up to the state by Al Capone as a sacrifice, taking the fall for Jack Zuta, a racketeer who ran a string of whorehouses, but who was already dead by the time the trial wrapped up.

It seemed that everyone had a motive to kill Jake Lingle, but crime historians are in general agreement that Brothers took the rap and served time for a substantial cash payoff. Still, we'll never really know for sure.

After his release in 1940, Brothers returned to St. Louis, beat his original murder case and became hooked up with the local mob. Three months after an abortive attempt on his life, Leo Brothers died of heart disease in St. Louis on December 23, 1950. He took the secrets of the Lingle murder with him to the grave.

MURDER OF JUDGE FETZER

On October 26, 1935, three attorneys were seated quietly inside one of the law offices fronting a bank of elevators in the center of the Ashland Block building, located at Clark and Randolph Streets in downtown Chicago. The Ashland Block was one of the most populous commercial centers in the Chicago Loop and was filled with lawyers, architects and designers.

On this particular day, it was the noon hour, and the receptionist had just gone to lunch. The attorneys suddenly heard the discharge of a gun coming from down the hall. Seconds later, the doors to the office were thrown open and a red-haired man burst through them. He brandished an automatic pistol in his hand. The gunman hurried into the office and, stopping short of an inner doorway, aimed his gun at attorney William Hawthorne, who stared at the stranger in shocked disbelief. Before Hawthorne had a chance to speak or flee, the stranger opened fire, and two bullets pierced the lawyer's back and head. He fell to the floor mortally wounded. A second attorney, Bert Lannon, slammed the door shut, while Charles Horgan, another lawyer who shared offices with the other men, frantically pushed pieces of furniture against the door, hoping that the gunman would not be able to get inside.

Horgan grabbed the telephone and tried to call the police. Moments later, he and Lannon heard another shot, followed by another. They cautiously opened the door and saw the stranger who had shot William

Randolph Street in 1900. On the left are the Powers' Theatre, the Sherman House and Burnham and Root's round-bayed Ashland Block, where the shooting of Judge Fetzer occurred. All of these buildings have since been demolished.

Hawthorne lying on the floor. Blood was slowly pooling from under his fallen body.

Less than five minutes earlier, the red-haired man, who proved to be a forty-two-year-old epilepsy sufferer and ex-convict named Raymond Lanning, had casually walked into the twelfth-floor law offices of Judge William R. Fetzer. He asked to see the judge, but stenographer Florence Levy told him that Fetzer was busy at the moment. Lanning, who was nicely dressed in a brown suede coat and was carrying a portfolio, introduced himself and chatted casually with Levy. He was calm and composed, and his attitude offered no hint about the deadly rampage that he was about to unleash.

When the unsuspecting Judge Fetzer and a downtown attorney named Nathan Weintroob emerged from the inner office, Lanning seemed to snap. He pulled a .32-caliber automatic from the pocket of his coat and fired two shots into Fetzer before dropping the portfolio that he had carried into the office. He then turned the gun toward Weintroob. "You don't like me either, so I'll kill you, too!" he shrieked. Lanning then ran down the hall, firing several wild shots before shooting William Hawthorne in his law office. A few moments later, he shot himself.

After the police had arrived and the smoke had cleared from the inexplicable rampage, Lanning was taken to the Bridewell Prison infirmary, which was located at West Twenty-sixth Street and California Avenue. When he arrived there, doctors removed a suicide note from the dying man's pocket. His motive for the slaughter was plainly spelled out. He had written:

> *A too severe judge, sticking to the letter of the law and ignoring human principles, has taken my life, his own through me, and the lives of several others, perhaps through me. I too, am severe, cruel now, because I find the majority of people that way.*

Judge Fetzer, who had sentenced Lanning to Bridewell six years earlier for criminal assault with a knife, had become the victim of a vengeance killer—a man who had long years in his cell to brood over the injustices that he believed had been done to him.

Lanning, who had a long record of most minor offenses, had been released from the custody of the psychiatric ward only a few weeks before the attack. During his incarceration, he blamed his epileptic seizures on Fetzer. He spent his time writing a convoluted and bizarre eighty-five-page autobiographical manuscript called "Rust," which he eventually hoped to publish with a literary magazine. The title of his manuscript referred to Lanning's perception that Fetzer was "eating away" at his life. In the rambling story, he vowed to carry out the assassinations of Judge Fetzer, Chicago mayor Edward J. Kelly and anti-vice crusader Reverend Phillip Yarrow. He also vowed to burn down the Union Stockyards.

Whether Lanning actually intended to carry out these acts or if they were merely the wild fantasies of a deranged mind will never be known, but he did kill Judge Fetzer, which had been first on his list. Lanning's sister, Gloria, told the police that her brother had been suffering from seizures ever since his wartime service. He acted queerly at times, she said, but he had never spoken badly about or made any threats toward Judge Fetzer. She said that he was a brilliant man and had done a lot of writing. When he was himself again, he would have been devastated by what he had done. She added, "It's better that he died."

The Ashland Block rampage was obviously a tragedy, but Judge Fetzer turned out to be a juicy victim in the case, at least as far as the newspapers were concerned.

William R. Fetzer was elected Seventh Ward alderman in 1917 after a bitter election battle with Professor Charles E. Merriman, a failed reformer and a political idealist from the University of Chicago. With the backing of downtown political operators loyal to Mayor William Hale Thompson, Fetzer was declared the winner by just three votes following a recount. Since the election was held in Chicago, one can only wonder if those three voters were dead or alive!

At the start of the Prohibition era, Fetzer was elected to (or possibly bought) a seat on the municipal court bench in 1920. He was at best a machine judge of dubious distinction, drawing both the attention of the Chicago Crime Commission and the Chicago Bar Association for releasing gangsters and for discharging a suspected bomber who was arrested with one hundred pounds of dynamite in his possession.

In 1921, observing the proceedings in Fetzer's courtroom, a Crime Commission court observer who was keeping tabs on suspected judicial bribe takers noted, "The judge uses technicalities as a pretense to excuse guilty persons. Judge is too lenient. So many fixers are prominent that city prosecutor Bombaugh in the court said he was ashamed of it."

A rumor spread that claimed Fetzer was a "syndicate judge," a mob mouthpiece who protected big-shot hoods from prosecution, while coming down harshly on small-time offenders like Lanning so that he could create an image that he was a dedicated crime fighter and a friend of the people for the benefit of the voters.

The judge earned the nickname "Cash Register" Fetzer for payoffs received from professional bondsmen who loitered inside his chambers. For this and other misdeeds during his years on the bench, he was often severely criticized by Chief Justice Harry Olson. Fetzer released scores of syndicate gunmen accused of racketeering and running gambling operations in the terrible Maxwell Street district, where the Genna brothers ruled for years. In September 1930, Fetzer received unwanted publicity for a decision in which he held that betting on a horse race was not a game of chance but of skill.

When he was killed, the press described "Cash Register" Fetzer's career as a "stormy" one. It was the best adjective that reporters could come up with while still satisfying their editors, who had ordered them to put together a respectful review of the judge's life and times filled with guarded praise.

Fetzer was given a funeral with full Masonic honors at Oakwood Cemetery on the South Side. He was mourned by his friends and colleagues, and just like so many Chicago gangsters who had been buried in consecrated ground, his death elevated the sinner to a saint.

ONLY A MATTER OF TIME

THE INEVITABLE MURDER OF JOSEPH BOLTON

When looking back at the lives of some murder victims, it sometimes seems as if they were inevitably destined to come to a violent end. This is not a case of passing judgment on the way they lived their lives or dismissing their deaths by saying that they deserved to be murdered; rather, it is a wish that they could have seen the warning signs that are so clear to us in hindsight.

One such unlucky person was Joseph W. Bolton Jr., a mild-mannered Chicago businessman who was apparently scheduled to be murdered at the moment he got married.

Bolton was married in 1922. His wife, Mildred, was a troubled woman at the start of their marriage and became even more unhinged as the years passed. She was suspicious and possessive of Bolton and always imagined him with other women. Of course, nothing could have been further from the truth. Mildred had been the only woman Bolton had ever dated, and the tall, bespectacled man was so shy and docile that he found it almost impossible to carry on a conversation with any woman for more than a few minutes. Mildred persisted in her fantasies, though, believing that her husband was a seducer of every female he came across. She punished him for his imaginary transgressions, and she made his life a living hell.

Bolton was a successful insurance broker, but his business began to suffer because of Mildred's strange behavior. She often barged into his office and accused him of having affairs with the secretaries who

Joseph Bolton, the man who spent his entire married life knowing that someday his wife would murder him.

Mildred Bolton believed that no Cook County jury would convict a woman for killing her husband. She was wrong.

worked there, with other women he did business with and even with the wives of his friends. She began to show up and cause trouble at the office so often that eventually he was asked to resign, and Bolton went into business for himself. The couple moved to Chicago in 1928.

Eventually, Mildred's verbal attacks became physical altercations. She would often beat and slap her husband in public, knocking his glasses off his face and stepping on them. She even attacked him with knives and razors. The police were called to their home on several occasions, but Mildred always managed to convince them that things had just been blown out of proportion.

On July 22, 1934, police officer Joseph Lynch was called to a drugstore in Hyde Park at 3:00 a.m. When he arrived, he found Bolton almost unconscious as a druggist bandaged his right forearm, which had been viciously slashed. Bolton would give no statement to the police as he was moved to the hospital. Officer Lynch followed a trail of blood that ran from the pharmacy to a location two blocks away, 5230 University Avenue. When he rang the bell, Mildred Bolton answered the door and invited him into the parlor. Lynch asked her how her husband had come to be slashed, and she told him that Joseph had cut himself while shaving.

Needless to say, Officer Lynch was skeptical about how Bolton could have cut his arm while shaving at three o'clock in the morning, so he took Mildred with him to the hospital, where her husband was being stitched up. Bolton refused to admit that Mildred had attacked him.

By that time, Bolton must have known that his days were numbered. On January 20, 1936, he filed for divorce from Mildred. He simply couldn't take it anymore and cited his wife's cruelty as the reason for the separation.

Mildred wasted no time in seeking recourse. She purchased a .32-caliber revolver and six bullets on June 11 from the Hammond Loan Company, a pawnshop. Four days later, she called on her husband at his tenth-floor office at 166 West Jackson Boulevard. Shots rang out in the office. Andrea Houyoux, Bolton's secretary, rushed to the elevator and begged the operator to take her downstairs. After he did, Lincoln Knutson, the elevator operator, and Fred Ferguson, an electrician in the building, raced the elevator back up to the tenth floor.

They found Bolton writhing and beating his legs on the hallway floor. Blood was pooled beneath him, but he was still alive and conscious. Mildred stood casually in Bolton's open office door, the pistol in her hand. Bolton gasped to the building employees, "Keep that woman away from me!"

Mildred merely smiled before she spoke, "Why don't you get up and stop faking?" As Ferguson rushed past her, running to get a doctor for Bolton, she called after him, "Don't you mind! He's just putting on an act!"

Of course, it was not an act. Bolton had been shot several times, and he was removed to a doctor's office, where physicians tried to save his life. Mildred stood around, making odd remarks and kissing her dying husband's brow. Bolton died within the hour, and Mildred was arrested.

Initially, Mildred denied shooting her husband. She claimed that she had never touched the gun and that Bolton had shot himself—despite the fact that two of the bullets had been fired into his back.

While she was in jail awaiting trial, Mildred became a questionable sort of celebrity. She earned the nickname of "Marble Mildred" when she calmly proclaimed that "they don't convict women in Cook County for killing their husbands." She received hundreds of pounds of fan mail. One housewife wrote, "You should have killed him whether you did it or not." Another letter writer stated, "If I had the nerve, I would have killed mine ten years ago." Another woman wrote, "Mildred, you are a saint and the jury will acquit you with orchids. A group of us is planning to celebrate your day of liberty with a dinner party and we want you to be our guest of honor."

Eventually, Mildred admitted that she had shot her husband. She had intended to kill herself, she said, and had gone to Bolton's office to commit suicide. Instead, the two of them had argued, he had called her a "vile name" and she shot him. When the case went to trial, Prosecutor William F. Crowley went after her with everything he had. He told the jury:

> *If you want to protect American manhood, if you want to protect the lives of husbands and businessmen from nagging, contemptible, vicious creatures to whom they might be married, I implore you, gentlemen, to consider this case calmly and deliberately and give her what she deserves—the electric chair.*

The jury spent only thirty-seven minutes in deliberations, casting three ballots. On the first, they decided that Mildred was guilty, and during the next two votes, they sentenced her to death. She became the first woman in Illinois history to be sentenced to die in the electric chair.

The judge set July 23 as the date for motions for a new trial, and Mildred returned to her cell for an evening meal of vegetable soup, bread, coffee and a cup of cocoa. She was placed on suicide watch, just in case she, as the newspapers put it, "decided to cheat the chair by suicide."

When Mildred returned to court, her case was automatically appealed. Judge Robert C. O'Connell, an advocate against the death penalty, forced Mildred to accept the appeal, even though she didn't want it. "There's no use of another trial. I haven't a chance, and besides, I think the verdict is right," she said.

However, under the law, any case that involved capital punishment had to be referred to the state supreme court, whether the defendant wanted it or not. Mildred's public defender, Benjamin Bachrach, worked on the appeal, even though his client still hoped for her October 29 death date. His argument was that the jury's verdict was the result of class prejudice against husband killers.

Mildred understood the prejudice. "I got what I deserved," she said.

When the case went to the Supreme Court, the appeal was denied, and Mildred was sentenced to die on February 26, 1937. However, a last-minute reprieve from Illinois governor Henry Horner saved her life. The governor commuted the death sentence to 199 years in prison with no parole just three hours before she was to be executed.

Some suggested that Mildred had been spared because she was a woman. In keeping with her nickname of "Marble Mildred," she calmly told newspaper reporters, "I detest women who hide behind their sex. I have no adequate words to express my feelings. I still have no fear of death and never did have."

Mildred was sent to serve out her sentence at the women's penitentiary in Dwight, but she only lived a few more years. She died in her cell on August 29, 1943, committing suicide by cutting her wrists with a pair of stolen scissors. She left a brief note behind, which read, "I wish to die as I have lived, completely alone."

She made no mention of the husband she had sent to an early grave. Perhaps he didn't matter in the greater scheme of things, for Joseph Bolton's days had been numbered from the moment Mildred agreed to be his wife.

"KISS OF DEATH" MCDONALD

MURDER AT THE PALACE THEATRE

Chicago has long been a city of theatres, and one of the most grand was the RKO Palace, which opened in October 1926 and was housed inside the Bismarck Hotel at the southeast corner of Randolph and LaSalle. The majestic theatre was the flagship of the Orpheum circuit until moving pictures replaced vaudeville in 1931. The theatre featured an orchestra pit, a dress circle and a balcony and was modeled after Louis XIV's Palace of Versailles in France. With the disappearance of the RKO studio name in the 1950s, the place simply became known the Palace, advertising modern innovations that carried it until it finally closed down in 1962. It reopened a few years later as the Bismarck, which featured a mix of movies and live performances, but it didn't last. The theatre finally closed for good in the 1980s, sadly forgotten and neglected.

Some came to believe that the old Palace was cursed in some way, doomed to not survive. It was suggested that where infamy occurred, bad luck was sure to follow. And it's not surprising that bad things could happen at the Palace. In the 1940s, for only sixty cents, a patron could spend the entire day and evening at the movies and never be forced to leave by an usher or floorwalker—one reason why many crooks and gunmen on the lam hid out in downtown movie houses.

But it was no small-time hoodlum who brought notoriety to the Palace Theatre. It was a young man named Clarence McDonald,

The Palace Theatre was located inside of the Bismarck Hotel.

who murdered his girlfriend because he didn't want anyone else to have her.

On the night of February 25, 1942, a teenage boy kissed his sweetheart goodbye and then killed her in the shadows of the darkened Palace Theatre. When asked several hours later why he did it, seventeen-year-old Clarence McDonald of west suburban Berwyn hesitated before he answered and then said, "I killed her because I didn't want anyone else to have her."

McDonald, a handsome blond youth, had fired a .38-caliber bullet into the head of pretty Dorothy Broz, just seconds after kissing her in a final gesture of love. Dorothy was a classmate of McDonald at J. Stirling Morton Township High School in Cicero and had been dating him on and off for some time. Although she used religious differences as an excuse, Dorothy called off the romance and abandoned her premature promises of marriage to McDonald because she had lost interest in the young man. Bright and ambitious, the girl had turned her enthusiasm toward college. She planned to attend either the University of Chicago or Steven's Beauty College in the Loop.

It became common knowledge to friends and classmates that McDonald did not take kindly to Dorothy breaking up with him. He often spoke harshly to her, had allegedly pointed an unloaded gun at her inside of Lanke's ice cream store in Cicero and, in a fit of anger, was rumored to have punched her in the face.

Why Dorothy would have gone on a date with McDonald to the Palace on the night of her death is unknown. Perhaps she was just too kindhearted to hurt her former boyfriend, or perhaps his constant pressure finally wore down her defenses. We'll never know for sure why she went, but on February 25, Dorothy agreed to attend a matinée at the Palace. They left the high school campus at 12:45 p.m. and arrived in the Loop about a half hour later. Dorothy and Clarence waited for the next show, killing time at the Carson Pirie Scott department store at State and Washington. They walked to the Palace a little before 2:00 p.m., just in time for the matinée show of *Hellzapoppin'*, a slapstick comedy starring Martha Raye and Olsen & Johnson, a popular vaudeville act.

They found seats together on the lower balcony, among fifteen hundred other theatregoers, and McDonald held on to the .38-caliber pistol that he had stolen from the Great Western Railway freight yard, where he had been employed as a messenger during the previous holiday season. He cradled the gun in his pocket, waiting for just the right time to use it.

At 4:26 p.m., following a newsreel, a crime noir picture called *Sealed Lips* began to roll through its opening credits. Two minutes later, during the clamor of on onscreen depiction of a prison riot, McDonald planted a kiss on Dorothy's lips and then pressed the muzzle of his handgun into the girl's left side.

Her shrill scream could barely be heard above the clamor of the action on screen, and the sound of the gunshot mixed into the sound of the gunshots in the film. Dorothy slumped over in her seat. McDonald stood up, composed himself and then quietly walked into the upper balcony, where he lost himself in the crowd. Lingering for just a moment, he stole one backward glance at Dorothy and then went down the stairs and exited the alley door of the theatre before anyone in the audience was even aware of what had occurred. A few eyewitnesses told the police that they assumed it was a promotional stunt tied in with the frantic, shoot-'em-up entertainment of *Hellzapoppin'*. By the time the police arrived and sealed off the exits, the killer was long gone.

McDonald caught the Douglas line elevated train at Quincy and Wells and returned to his sister's home. Either feeling no regret about what he had done or simply stunned by Dorothy's murder, he took in another double feature at the Olympic Theatre in Cicero with a friend from school. He returned home when the movies were over and went to bed after concealing the murder weapon in the garage behind the house.

At 3:45 a.m., the police came to the door. Investigators had been questioning Dorothy's friends and soon learned of McDonald's violent, possessive behavior. They also learned that his home life was a mess. Clarence's father had hanged himself in the Marquette District Police Station on September 3, 1936, after he was accused of raping his thirteen-year-old daughter, Phoebe. When Clarence was arrested, he wailed to the officers, "There's nothing more to live for since Dottie's dead." Fearing that he might choose his father's method of ending his life, the young man was placed on suicide watch in jail.

Later that same morning, McDonald was taken back to the Palace Theatre and was forced to reenact the shooting for the police, reporters and the county coroner. This was standard police procedure in those days. After this was over, McDonald gave a full confession to Captain Thomas Duffy in the interrogation room of the First District Police station. He told Duffy that he had thought of "doing away" with Dorothy for three days before he finally gathered the nerve and pulled the trigger. He didn't want anyone else to have his girl, but he was unsure how he was going to live without her. He told the press, "I wish they would give me the electric chair, I have nothing to live for now." Jaded reporters dubbed the young man "Kiss of Death" McDonald.

An inquest was held, and McDonald was present. During the proceedings, an outraged uncle of the dead girl attacked Clarence and punched him in the face. McDonald's sister, Mrs. Robert Wagner, pleaded for sympathy for the disturbed young man. She begged reporters to understand, stating, "He was full of hate and anger and it grew in him until he had to get it out in some way. He was taunted by a relative who repeatedly told him, 'Your father was insane and killed himself. Someday you will be insane, too!'"

During McDonald's trial, psychiatrists for both the defense and the prosecution examined the boy and testified about his state of mind before, during and after the murder. The only thing they seemed able to agree on was that he was a complete puzzle to them. The jury convicted him of murder on May 22, 1942. He was sentenced to life in prison. He managed to serve eighteen years of his original sentence at the reformatory in Pontiac, Illinois, and was paroled on March 17, 1961. After leaving the prison gates behind him, he vanished into history.

DEATH OF A GANGSTER POLITICIAN

The clock chimed midnight at the Randolph Tower in downtown Chicago on October 8, 1948. Just outside of the revolving door that allowed access to the lobby, William Granata was hacked to death by two vicious swipes from a killer's meat cleaver. The forty-two-year-old Republican candidate for circuit court clerk never saw his assassin coming. The steel of the cleaver slammed into his skull and then cut his jugular vein. He collapsed on the pavement, likely gasping for air and trying to croak out a few last words that no one was around to hear. At that hour, the normally busy intersection of Wells Street and Randolph was nearly deserted. A full five minutes passed before the Randolph Tower elevator man, Nick Salm, tried to come to the fallen man's rescue. By that time, Granata was lying in a pool of blood and it was too late for medical assistance. He was pronounced dead upon arrival at Henrotin Hospital.

When Granata's twenty-eight-year-old wife, Violet, arrived at the hospital, she was nearly incoherent. As she wept, she shouted at the reporters who had gathered when they heard about the murder. Being led away from her husband's bloody body she cried, "It should have been Sheriff Walsh, not him!" She was referring to Elmer Walsh, her husband's friend and political sponsor and the only political figure in Cook County history to ever defeat Richard J. Daley in an election. Granata had skillfully managed Walsh's election win over the up-and-coming Daley, who would eventually rule Chicago as mayor for twenty-one years. The sheriff later responded to Violet's statement, "I can't imagine what she meant. William Granata was a clean-cut fellow if there ever was one. Granata was a capable lawyer. He and his brother Peter are powerful in West Side politics. I'm at a complete loss as to why anyone would want to kill such a fine fellow."

The police department was at a loss to explain it also. Chief of Detectives Walter Storms assigned twenty of his best men to work the case, but mob murders of this kind are never solved in Chicago, whether by accident or by design.

Sheriff Elmer Walsh had told reporters that the Granata brothers were powerful in West Side politics, but this was a gross understatement. William Granata's rise to power was one of thousands of stories that came out of the poor Italian immigrant neighborhoods on the near West Side. When he was barely past his fifth birthday, he was sent out to peddle newspapers at Van Buren and Franklin Streets, while his widowed mother, Rose, continued her late husband's import-export business from their family home in the poorest section of the Italian quarter. In spite of the family's extreme living conditions, William did well in school and completed his law school studies at De Paul and Northwestern.

Hard on the coattails of his older brother, Peter, who was elected to the state legislature from the Seventeenth District, Granata became active in Republican politics as a young man. In 1940, he received a patronage appointment from Governor Dwight Green to lead the Illinois Industrial Commission. At the time of his death, he was the Republican committeeman of the Twenty-seventh Ward, a very important post in city politics since the committeeman controlled all of the jobs and local appointments. In other words, he could get just about any sort of favor that he needed from anyone who was looking for a city job for themselves, a friend or a relative.

Before thousands of southern African Americans began pouring into the Twenty-seventh Ward in the 1940s and began electing candidates more favorable to their interests, the ward was a nest of syndicate gangsters and a bloody battleground that had witnessed more than one assassination of a political fixer who didn't vote the way the mob wanted. The Granatas were well aware of the potential danger of their positions. In order to maintain their hold on power, the brothers formed an uneasy alliance with the West Side Bloc, a band of gangster-politicians who controlled patronage, appointments, gambling and all other vices in nine crucial West Side wards from the era of Al Capone through the 1970s. The bloc sponsored Democratic aldermen in Chicago and Republican legislators in Springfield, all of whom were guaranteed to vote the way it wanted. The bloc consistently voted down any piece of legislation that threatened vice in Chicago. Anyone who dared to stand in its way was likely to find himself in an early grave.

Operating through the long corrupt First Ward, the bloc delivered large voter turnouts to any cooperative politician who was willing to go along with it. State Representative James Anducci, who was arrested eighteen times between 1920 and 1934, was the boss of the Seventeenth District for the West Side mobsters. Anducci, a close friend of gangster "Dago" Lawrence Mangano, was elected to the state legislature for the first time in 1934. His colorful arrest record didn't do anything to slow him down.

While Peter Granata cooperated with Anducci, William was not always so willing to go along. In fact, he had to be warned several times that his leanings toward reform were not appreciated. Anducci's brother, Joe, once told him, "Watch yourself, you're getting too big for your pants!"

So, who killed William Granata? The police didn't know, or they weren't looking very hard. A rumor spread that investigators had recovered a list of thirteen names from the dead man's pocket, and while the "mystery list" caused quite a stir in the morning papers, stories that it might be a list of potential killers was quickly quashed by Sheriff Walsh. He reported that the list contained only the names of "special deputy sheriffs" sponsored by Granata. The tradition of awarding badges and guns to unqualified political hacks and civilians who donated generously to the sheriff's election campaign went back many years in Cook County and continued, much to the embarrassment of many, through the 1990s.

The police interrogated Granata's driver, Amoth C. Cope, a Republican precinct worker with a record of petty crimes, as the last man to have seen Granata alive. Cope told officers that he had driven his boss to several dances and political rallies in three West Side wards that night before dropping him off in front of Randolph Tower, where he lived in an apartment with his wife and four-year-old son on the forty-second floor. Cope recalled the last thing he saw: "Granata got out in front of his place, waved to me, then crossed the street for his paper. I drove to Ogden and Madison for coffee and later dropped into several Madison Street taverns to talk with my precinct workers."

There were reports that three men were seen cruising around the block a short time before Granata was killed. A large butcher knife was left behind in a cab by a "mystery woman" and found by three youths who climbed into the taxi at Randolph and Wells just minutes after the murder. Police determined that the knife was not used in the murder but surmised that it had been brought along just in case something went wrong in the carrying out of the execution. The coroner believed that the meat cleaver had been wielded by a powerfully built man, who, of course, was never found.

Theories and a knife that might or might not have been part of the murder were all that ever emerged from the month-long investigation into Granata's slaying. It was assumed, however, that the killing was somehow linked to Granata's unwillingness to trade votes and grant influence to Jake Guzik and Paul "the Waiter" Ricca, who had taken control of the Capone syndicate after the death of Frank Nitti in 1943.

The course of the next weeks, months and years showed that things were still business as usual in Chicago. A few weeks after the murder, Granata's driver, Amoth Cope, went to work for James Anducci as his full-time chauffeur and lackey. Peter Granata remained embroiled in the West Side Bloc for many more years, until the group's power bases were finally eroded by increasing numbers of African Americans and Hispanics who refused to elect any more white gangsters to political office.

The murder of William Granata was never solved.

THE KILLER IN THE
LUMBERJACK COAT

When the body was discovered by a maid who had gone to tidy up a room in a downtown Chicago hotel, she reported it to the manager, Raymond Witaske, who locked the door and telephoned the Chicago Avenue police station. Nothing in the room had been disturbed when Lieutenant Jimmy Lynch and Sergeant John Ascher of the homicide detail walked into the room, but they quickly realized that they had a mystery on their hands.

It was a case that led from Chicago to New York to Seattle to Michigan and back again and involved a mysterious killer in a checkered lumberjack coat.

When the two police officers walked into the hotel room on the morning of December 30, 1948, the stale smell of cigarette smoke was still hanging in the air. The room contained a bed, a dresser, a small table and a lavatory. On the bed, lying faceup, was the naked body of an attractive red-haired woman who looked to be about thirty years old. She had been gagged with a wad of tissues and cloth. A piece of torn bedsheet was knotted around her throat and lashed to the bed. Her ankles were tied together, and another strip of cloth was around her wrists, binding them to her right thigh. There were no marks of violence on the woman's pale skin, and the detectives surmised that she had likely offered no resistance to being tied and gagged. Lieutenant Lynch knew this meant that she had probably been unconscious before she was tied up, possibly drugged.

On the floor next to the bed were about twenty cigarette butts. Instead of being put out when they were dropped, they had been tossed down carelessly and allowed to smolder, searing small holes in the carpet. It appeared that the killer had sat on the edge of the bed and chain-smoked while he watched the woman die.

Sergeant Ascher searched the room and found two empty whiskey bottles in the trash basket. On the dresser were two whiskey glasses, each containing the remnants of one last drink. Nearby, a woman's black purse was standing open. The purse contained little. There was a business card, bearing the name Seaton Allen, with a business address and telephone number in New York, and a change purse with thirty-six cents in it. Next to the purse were several matchbooks, with matches missing from all of them. Lynch noted that they came from various taverns and nightclubs along North Clark Street.

Jack Ross, a night clerk at the hotel, said that the red-haired woman had entered with a man, who had previously visited the hotel and registered under the names "Mr. and Mrs. Tom Morris." They had gone upstairs about 7:00 p.m. on the previous evening, and then, about 10:30 p.m., the woman had left alone. She had been followed by the man a few minutes later, and then the pair had returned together about 1:30 a.m.

About 2:00 a.m., Ross said that Morris had been patched through the switchboard and called the bus station. Then he called the desk and asked for a wake-up call at 8:00 a.m. Ross made the call himself, and Morris was downstairs in just a few minutes. He described the man as clean looking, with thick, dark, wavy hair that was combed back from his forehead. He stood about six feet tall and weighed about 175 pounds. He wore a dark blue suit and a white shirt, but instead of a standard overcoat, he wore a red and black checkered lumberjack coat.

Meanwhile, Sergeant Roy Holland had been talking to others who had rooms on the floor. One woman recalled that she had seen the couple in the hallway about 1:30 a.m. She remembered hearing the girl mention that she needed to catch a bus but recalled nothing else of the conversation. She said the hotel seemed very quiet after 2:00 a.m.

Deputy Coroner Cornelius Dore told the detectives that there was a very good reason that things were so quiet after 2:00 a.m., because this was about the time the red-haired woman had died. He examined the body and said that it appeared she had slowly strangled to death. However, there was not a mark of any kind on her neck, not even a small bruise. He carefully untied her wrists, and on the right finger, detectives noted a plain gold wedding band. Dore removed it and handed it to Lynch. He said, "Maybe the man really was her husband, but I'll bet his name wasn't Morris."

Detective Joe Ponicki was also searching the room. He found the woman's dress and coat in the closet. There was nothing to indentify the dress, but the coat bore the label of a Chicago manufacturer. The manufacturer, unfortunately, turned out not to be of any help. The coat was a stock model sold in shops all over the country, and it could have been purchased in any of them.

Sergeant Tom Laffey, headquarters fingerprint expert, examined the room for prints but only found two good ones on the whiskey bottle.

The investigators seemed to have few leads, but one they did have was the bus station. There definitely seemed to be a bus trip mixed up in the case somewhere, so Lieutenant Lynch sent Detective Ponicki down to the bus station to see what he could find out. After he left, the body was taken to the county morgue for an autopsy, and the rest of the detectives returned to headquarters.

Ponicki headed to the bus station. He reasoned that, in December, when most men wore overcoats, a man in a lumberjack coat would stand out. He was right, and he quickly found a man at a ticket window who remembered him. The man, Morris, had brought in a through ticket from New York to Seattle. He still had the unused portion from Chicago to Seattle. He told the station agent that he had changed his mind about continuing his trip and wanted to trade it in. He bought a ticket to Flint, Michigan, and received the difference, about thirty dollars, in cash.

Ponicki checked the man's description with the ticket agent, and there was little doubt that it was the same man. Then, Ponicki checked with redcaps, porters and loaders but was unable to find anyone who remembered the man actually boarding a bus.

When Ponicki reported this, Lieutenant Lynch suggested that perhaps the man had not actually left town. He might have purchased the ticket just to throw investigators off the trail, knowing that they would check the bus station. He also surmised that Morris might have gone to Detroit, so the police in both Michigan cities were sent a bulletin with the man's description and asked to pick him up if he appeared there.

At headquarters, Sergeant Ascher had been thinking about the description of the man calling himself Tom Morris. It sounded very much like a local hood Ascher was familiar with named Nick Andrews, who frequented taverns near the bus station. At a tavern where Ascher had often seen the man, he talked to a bartender who told him that Andrews had not been around for about a week, but he agreed to notify the homicide detective if he did come in.

Meanwhile, Lieutenant Lynch was working to try to identify the mysterious victim. He decided to call the number that was on the business card found in the woman's purse. He hoped that Seaton Allen would be able to provide a clue as to who the woman was. He called the man at his New York office.

Allen told the investigator everything that he knew about the girl. He had met her just the week before, on Christmas Eve, while having dinner in a nice restaurant. The girl told him that she had come to New York from Seattle almost a year before. Like so many other young women, she had hoped to find a good job in the city. But her dreams had soon been shattered. She found a job but made hardly enough to pay for her studio apartment. She was broke and homesick and had spent the last of her money on a holiday dinner. Allen had learned that she desperately wanted to go home to Seattle. Feeling sorry for her, he had given her enough money to buy a one-way bus ticket to Seattle. He had seen her off at the station that same evening.

Allen said that her name was Evangeline Storms Baker and that she had been divorced from William T. Baker of Sultan, Washington, only a short time before she came to New York.

This was all that Allen could tell Lynch, but it turned out to be enough. He immediately contacted the Seattle police, who located William Baker. From him, they obtained photographs of his former wife, and they were sent by airmail to Chicago. When they eventually arrived, it was clear that the body in the morgue was that of Evangeline Storms Baker.

A short time later, an autopsy report was sent to the Chicago Avenue station that revealed how the woman had been murdered so peacefully. At least one of her drinks, possibly more, had been laced with drugs. She had been unconscious when she was bound, gagged and likely raped. The drug had not been what killed her, though; she had definitely been slowly strangled.

Detective Ponicki continued working the streets. Using the matchbooks that had been found in the room, he began canvassing the Clark Street bars and clubs. The man in the lumberjack coat had been seen in all of them, usually with a woman. One man with whom the detective spoke particularly remembered the red-haired girl because she had talked to him. She had left her escort at a table and had started toward the restroom. She met this man and appealed to him for help, asking him to take her out of the bar. Fearing that her plea was some sort of setup for robbery, he brushed her off, but he did tell Ponicki that he had watched the girl after that. She had spoken to at least two other men, but apparently they had also denied her appeal for help. It seemed clear that she was afraid of the man in the lumberjack coat and that she had tried in vain to get away from him.

Joe Ponicki continued his canvass and found taverns on Wabash Avenue where the man in the lumberjack coat had also been seen. In some of them, he was identified as Nick Andrews, the man Ponicki was familiar with. In one place, near the bus station, the bartender said that a man fitting the description of the suspect had been there with the girl. She became sick after a few drinks and left with him. The bartender didn't know either one of them by name.

On January 7, 1949, eight days after the murder, Nick Andrews was picked up. He was wearing his usual red and black–checkered lumberjack coat at the time. When he was questioned as to his whereabouts, he told detectives that he had been out of town, but he wouldn't tell them where. He was unable to give a satisfactory account of his movements on the night of the crime. Questioned about Evangeline Baker, he denied that he had ever seen her and insisted that he knew nothing about her murder. He was held for further questioning, but detectives were sure that they had their man.

Strangely, on that same day, a man using the name John Wagner presented a check for thirty dollars to a hotel clerk in Detroit. The clerk excused himself on the pretext of going to the safe for the money but called the police instead. Taken into custody, Wagner insisted that the check was good. Of course, that was not why he had been picked up.

When he walked into the hotel lobby, Wagner, a tall man with dark, combed-back hair, was wearing a red and black lumberjack coat. Detroit police compared his description with the wanted notice they had received from Chicago and were sure that they had the man Windy City cops were looking for. A call was placed to Chicago, and detectives flew to Detroit, picked up Wagner and returned to Illinois.

Meanwhile, various witnesses had been rounded up and had viewed Nick Andrews in a lineup. They all agreed that he resembled the man they had seen with the redhead, but they couldn't be sure if it was him. Andrews continued to protest his innocence, although he refused to take a polygraph test and still refused to say where he had been for the past week.

The investigators were stumped and figured that it was worth a shot to have the witnesses take a look at John Wagner when he was brought in from Detroit. He was first viewed by Jack Ross, the hotel clerk, and was immediately recognized as the man who had claimed to be Tom Morris. Other witnesses were brought in, and each positively identified him as the man who had been seen with Evangeline Baker.

When confronted by these identifications, Wagner broke and confessed his crime. He had met the girl when she had stopped over in Chicago on her trip to Seattle. She had accepted his invitation to have a drink to celebrate Christmas. Wagner thought she had money and planned to rob her. He slipped drugs into one of her drinks, but instead of knocking her out, it just made her sick. He suggested that she go up to his hotel room and get some rest. Once in the room, though, the girl revived and, realizing that he was up to something, left. Wagner followed her, caught up with her and induced her into a tavern for another drink. While there, she tried to get help from other men, but it was too late. Wagner had drugged her again, and she became violently ill. He managed to get her back to the hotel, and in the hallway, she gasped that she had to catch her bus to Seattle, a remark overheard by one of the other hotel guests.

He got Evangeline into the room and gave her more of the drug. This time, it worked and she passed out. Wagner searched her purse and, realizing that she had no money, decided to rape and kill her so that she could not identify him later. He undressed her, tied her up and, when he was finished with her, watched her slowly strangle to death as he smoked and finished off the whiskey. He took the bus ticket, the only thing the girl had that was worth anything, cashed it in and bought a ticket to Michigan.

He had absolutely no remorse for what he had done. John Wagner was a stone-cold killer. His fingerprints were matched to those on the whiskey bottle, and he was charged with Evangeline's murder. He was convicted in Cook County Criminal Court in September 1949 and sentenced to serve a life term at Menard Prison in Chester.

As for Nick Andrews, he was released after Wagner was charged with the murder. He never accounted for where he had been during the first week of January 1949, and as far as the detectives were concerned, he never had to. He was merely unlucky enough to bear a passing resemblance to a killer—and to have bad taste in coats.

BIBLIOGRAPHY

Adler, Jeffrey S. *First in Violence, Deepest in Dirt*. Cambridge, MA: Harvard University Press, 2006.

Asbury, Herbert. *Gem of the Prairie*. New York: Alfred A. Knopf, 1940.

Binder, John J. *The Chicago Outfit*. Chicago: Arcadia, 2003.

Chicago Historical Society

Chicago Public Library

Cowdery, Ray. *Capone's Chicago*. Lakeville, MN: Northstar Commemoratives, 1987.

Demaris, Ovid. *Captive City*. New York: Lyle Stuart, 1969.

Eghigian, Mars, Jr. *After Capone*. Nashville, TN: Cumberland House, 2006.

Everett, Marshall. *The Great Chicago Theater Disaster*. Chicago: Publisher's Union of America, 1904.

Farr, Finis. *Chicago*. New Rochelle, NY: Arlington House, 1973.

Griffith, William. *Fatal Drop*. Decatur, IL: Whitechapel Press, 2008.

Halper, Albert. *The Chicago Crime Book*. Cleveland: World Publishing, 1967.

Hatch, Anthony. *Tinderbox*. Chicago: Chicago Academy Publishers, 2003.

Helmer, William. *Public Enemies*. New York: Facts on File, 1998.

Helmer, William, and Arthur J. Bilek. *The St. Valentine's Day Massacre*. Nashville, TN: Cumberland House, 2004.

Helmer, William, and Rick Mattix. *The Complete Public Enemy Almanac*. Nashville, TN: Cumberland House, 2007.

Johnson, Curt, with R. Craig Sautter. *Wicked City*. Highland Park, IL: December Press; 1994.

Keefe, Rose. *Guns and Roses*. Nashville, TN: Cumberland House, 2003.

Lait, Jack, and Lee Mortimer. *Chicago Confidential*. New York: Crown Publishers, 1950.

Landesco, John. *Organized Crime in Chicago*. Chicago: University of Chicago Press, 1968.

Lesy, Michael. *Murder City*. New York: W.W. Norton & Co., 2007.

Lewis, Lloyd, and Henry Justin Smith. *Chicago*. New York: Harcourt, Brace & Co., 1929.

Lindberg, Richard. *Chicago by Gaslight*. Chicago: Chicago Academy Publishers, 1996.

———. *Return Again to the Scene of the Crime*. Nashville, TN: Cumberland House, 2001.

———. *Return to the Scene of the Crime*. Nashville, TN: Cumberland House, 1999.

Nash, Jay Robert. *Bloodletters and Bad Men*. New York: M. Evans and Company, Inc., 1995.

———. *Open Files*. New York: McGraw-Hill Book Co., 1983.

Sifakis, Carl. *Encyclopedia of American Crime*. New York: Facts on File, 1982.

Taylor, Troy. *Bloody Chicago*. Decatur, IL: Whitechapel Press, 2006.

———. *Bloody Illinois*. Decatur, IL: Whitechapel Press, 2008.

———. *Dead Men Do Tell Tales*. Decatur, IL: Whitechapel Press, 2008.

Wright, Sewell Peaslee. *Chicago Murders*. New York: Duell, Sloan & Pierce, 1945.

NEWSPAPERS

Chicago American
Chicago Daily News
Chicago Herald-American
Chicago Herald & Examiner
Chicago Inter-Ocean
Chicago Sun-Times
Chicago Times
Chicago Tribune

About the Author

Troy Taylor is the author of more than sixty books on history, crime, mysteries and the supernatural in America. He was born and raised in Illinois and currently resides in Decatur, Illinois, which was called "one of the most corrupt cities in the state" during the 1920s.

Visit us at
www.historypress.net